The Australian Geographic Book of

The Blue Mountains

Text by Peter Meredith • Photography by Don Fuchs

Cover: *Triple icon of the Blue Mountains, the Three Sisters are the eroded remnants of a narrow headland jutting into the Jamison Valley.*

Back cover: *The lush vegetation in the gardens at Withycombe, Mount Wilson, offer shady seclusion.*

Title page: *Rockclimbers pause after reaching the summit of the middle pinnacle of the Three Sisters.*

Contents page: *A new day dawns over Dunns Swamp, a wildlife haven and attractive car-camping area on the Cudgegong River on the western perimeter of Wollemi National Park.*

Page 2: *Canyoners prepare to tackle Kanangra Main in Kanangra-Boyd National Park. This series of waterfalls provides one of the most challenging canyoning experiences in Australia.*

Page 3: *Above the gorge where Fortress Creek tumbles into the Grose Valley walkers (top) are offered a spectacular view across to Lockley Pylon on the opposite ridge. Mt Banks is in the distance. A bushwalker (bottom) crosses a suspension bridge that takes the Six Foot Track over the Coxs River.*

Page 4: *Blue Mountains bush kaleidoscope. Clockwise from right: a gum tree after shedding its bark; characteristic markings on a scribbly gum; huntsman spider on scorched bark; beetle on gum.*

Page 5: *The eastern tiger snake is found throughout the Greater Blue Mountains region.*

The Great Zig Zag *(above) carried rail traffic up and down the western escarpment of the Blue Mountains from 1869 to 1910. After walking the Six Foot Track, bushwalker Barbara Montz (right) surveys Caves House at Jenolan.*

First published in 1999 by Australian Geographic Pty Ltd
PO Box 321, Terrey Hills NSW 2084, Australia
Phone: (02) 9450 2344, fax (02) 9450 2990
email: books@australiangeographic.com.au

Managing Director: Paul Gregory
Publisher: Howard Whelan
Production/Creative Director: Tony Gordon
Managing Editor, Books: Averil Moffat

Editor: Frank Povah
Design and Photographic Edit: Moyna Smeaton
Director of Cartography: Will Pringle
Production Manager: Jožica Črnčec
Picture Research: Lydia Twidle
Cartographers: Sue Dyhrberg and Land Information Centre
Proofreading: Harold Abrahams and Associates Pty Ltd
Editorial Assistants: Sandy Richardson, Michelle Thinius

Photography by Don Fuchs unless otherwise credited

Text © Australian Geographic
Photography © Australian Geographic

Printed in Australia by Inprint Pty. Ltd.

Copyright © Australian Geographic Pty Ltd 1999

National Library of Australia Cataloguing-in-Publication Data:

Meredith, Peter, 1946-.
    The Australian Geographic Book of the Blue Mountains.

    Includes index.
    ISBN 1 86276 026 8.

1. Blue Mountains (N.S.W.: Mountains) – Description and travel. 2.
Blue Mountains (N.S.W.: Mountains) – History. I. Fuchs, Donatus. II.
Australian Geographic Pty. Ltd. III. Title.

919.4450466

Acknowledgements
For their assistance with this book, Australian Geographic and Peter
Meredith would like to thank: Derek Murphy, Glenn Nash, Australian
School of Mountaineering; Jim Barrett; Gwen Silvey, Blue Mountains
Historical Society; Dalene Bennett, Daryl Buckingham, Wendy Dollin,
Margaret Webb, Blue Mountains Tourism Ltd; Bob Burton; Bygone
Beautys; Geoff Leach, Carrington Hotel; Margie Lowe, Caves House;
Debbie Low, City of Blue Mountains; Alex Colley, Keith Muir,
The Colong Foundation for Wilderness; Russell Cooper; David Alder,
Department of Mineral Resources; Trish Follenfant, Everglades
Gardens; Anne and Ian Smith, Falls Gallery; Don Folbigg; Helen and
Gary Ghent, "Withycombe"; Mark Cooper, Rod Gurney, Hartley Valley
4WD Club; Anne Southam, Hydro Majestic Hotel; Sharon Wellsted,
Imperial Hotel; John Callaghan, Jenolan Caves; Ernst Holland, Jenolan
Caves Reserve Trust; Geoff Bates, Phil Hammon, Katoomba Scenic
Railway and Skyway; Leonie Knapman; Val Lang; John Ekin, Leura
House; Val Lheude; Andy Macqueen; Rusty Worsman, Mount Tomah
Botanic Garden; Mary Reynolds, Mount Wilson Historical Group; NSW
National Parks and Wildlife Service (especially Ian Brown, Andrew
Cox, Kim de Govrick, Mick English, John Giles, Anthony Johnson,
Vickii Lett, Geoff Luscombe, Glen Morris, Chris Pavich and Vanessa
Richardson); Stirling Butchard, Newnes Hotel; Jane Lennon, Amanda
Trevillion, Norman Lindsay Gallery; Jenni Edmonds, Andrew Grant,
Powerhouse Museum; Peter Prineas; Jeff Rigby; Joanne Cross, Rover
Australia Pty Limited; Tim Entwisle, Royal Botanic Gardens Sydney;
Bill Shields; Rodney and Noelene Smith; John Lowe, Springwood
Historical Society; Anthony Stimson; Colin Judge, Sydney Water;
Patrick Thompson; Geoff Lillico, 3801 Ltd; Bill and Joan Tindale;
Victor Poljanski, State Rail Authority of New South Wales; Bert and
Bruce Sykes; Armstrong Osborne, University of Sydney; Peter Bishop,
Varuna Writers' Centre; Allan Wales; Haydn Washington; Allan
Watson; James Williamson; Victor Perry, Wonarua Tribal Council;
Norah Holman, Woodford Academy; Michael Forbes, Zig Zag
Railway Co-op Ltd.

Page 8: *Clockwise from top left: fly agaric mushrooms in
a colourful cluster at Mt Wilson; a grevillea, several species
of which grow in the Blue Mountains; the waratah, floral
emblem of NSW and one of Australia's best-known
wildflowers; sparkling after rain, a hairpin banksia glows
yellow among sombre foliage.*

Page 9: *The two-pronged fruit of the mountain devil,
a prickly shrub that grows in the Blue Mountains and
throughout NSW, gives the plant its name. The fruit
are frequently made into devil dolls for the tourist trade.*

Opposite: *Empress Falls, one of the many beautiful
cascades created by Valley of Waters Creek as it tumbles
into the valley between the townships of Leura and
Wentworth Falls. This is a popular canyoning site.*

Contents

Map of the Blue Mountains   14

Foreword   15
   by Howard Whelan

Introduction   17

Kanangra country   21
   Wilderness of the far south

A lake and a river   43
   Lake Burragorang and the Kowmung River

Edge of eternity   61
   The lower mountains

City in the mountains   79
   Historic settlement of crags and vistas

Wild depths, horticultural heights   101
   The Grose Valley

"A scene of great wildness"   123
   The western edge of Wollemi

The middle of nowhere   139
   Wollemi's north and east

Index   158

Further reading   160

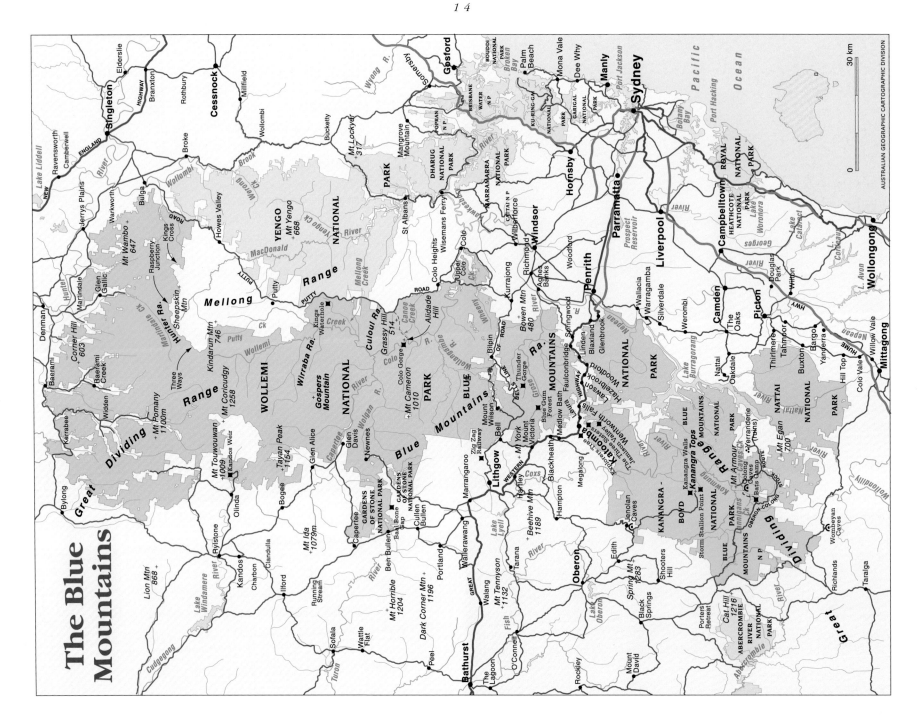

The Blue Mountains

It's been 20 years since my first foray into the Blue Mountains. Having just arrived in Sydney, I'd ventured into a tiny outdoor shop called Paddy Pallins and picked up a brochure for a company called Blue Mountains Expeditions. It promised abseiling into narrow, water-filled gorges, rock climbing on sandstone walls and bushwalking along remote creeks that promised refreshing swims in long, dark pools.

The brochure was so well-presented that I was sure Blue Mountains Expeditions must be a very big company. In fact, it was run by two teenaged entrepreneurs, Ken and Richard Rosebery, who invited me along as guest journalist on some of their trips. Little did they know what a profound impact that invitation would have.

Over the next few months I joined them for li-lo trips down the Wollangambe River, abseils into Claustral Canyon and bushwalks to the Blue Gum Forest where we'd heat up our jaffle-iron to cook breakfast while the sun fired the Grose Valley's upper clifflines.

On those trips I began to understand the details beneath the Blue Mountains' grandeur. I experienced the heart-stopping rustle of leaf litter as big goannas escaped up the far side of gum trees, was mesmerised

LYDIA TWIDLE

by bad banksia men lit up by a flickering campfire and as for lyrebirds, they seemed the cleverest birds on Earth. Slowly and irrevocably, the Blue Mountains sank its hooks into me.

For many people today, the Blue Mountains are little more than beguiling views from either the Great Western Highway or the Bells Line of Road as they travel from the Sydney basin to the Great Western Plains and back. I was fortunate to have had

the benefit of local knowledge to guide me into understanding this special part of Australia and often wondered if it would be possible to create a guidebook that would offer newcomers the same advantage. Thanks to the efforts of author Peter Meredith and photographer Don Fuchs, *The Australian Geographic Book of the Blue Mountains* does more than introduce the wonders of this region; it puts them into an historical and cultural context.

Peter worked as staff writer and associate editor for AUSTRALIAN GEOGRAPHIC over an eight-year stint, helping shape the style and standard of writing in what has become Australia's most popular geographical journal. In this book Peter captures not only the beautiful wilderness of the Blue Mountains, but the wonderful culture of those who have made it their home.

Whether you're a seasoned bushwalker or simply someone looking for a great excuse to escape modern day's frenetic pace, you'll find inspiration in the pages that follow. The next step, of course, will be to turn your reading into reality, and set off on your own journey of discovery.

Howard Whelan
Publisher

Introduction

Brilliant green patches of temperate rainforest, comprising mainly sassafras, coachwood, lilly pilly and some red cedar, stand out among the dense eucalypt bush shrouding the slopes of the Valley of the Waters beneath Wentworth Falls township. The valley, its dramatic sandstone cliffs and blue-tinged vistas create the kind of quintessential Blue Mountains scene that has mesmerised visitors since the early 1800s, among them naturalist Charles Darwin and explorer Paul de Strzelecki.

A railway bridge near my home gives an unobstructed view to the west. When I walk to the corner shop, I can never resist the temptation to stop and lean on the parapet and look 60 kilometres across Sydney's suburbs towards the ragged line on the horizon.

There aren't many places in Sydney where, on clear days, you can't get a view of the Blue Mountains. Glimpsed between high-rise buildings or from an urban ridge, they suddenly surprise you; and if you work on the western side of a tower block, you can take in the sweep of 100 km of mountain range.

Like the sea, mountains inspire and lure. Sydneysiders are doubly inspired and lured, with the Tasman Sea to their east and the Blue Mountains in the west. When you fly into Sydney, you notice a blue-green expanse on the city's western edge extending for 200 km on a north–south axis and covering more than 10,000 sq. km. You may wonder, as I did on first arriving in Sydney, what so much bush is doing right next to one of the world's major metropolises.

Down on the ground, the mountains look like nothing more than a line of gentle hills. That's one of their great deceptions. The other is that they are neither hills nor mountains but a plateau, up to 85 km wide and sloping from more than 1300 metres at its highest point in the west to less than

400 m on its eastern escarpment. Over aeons, rivers and creeks have cut down through the plateau, wearing away the sandstone and creating the spectacular gullies, gorges, canyons, mesas, ridges and prominent peaks that characterise the region today.

Scientists believe that for thousands of years the Blue Mountains acted as a buffer between Aboriginal groups living east and west of the range. But it wasn't an impassable barrier: there is plenty of evidence that Aboriginal people crossed the mountains on a network of well-trodden tracks.

This may not have been immediately obvious to Australia's European colonists. Escaped convicts were probably the first to penetrate the range's incomprehensible depths, believing that some kind of El Dorado lay beyond. That is always the way with mountains: they foster dreams of fabulous realms on the far side.

It was this dream that inspired the early explorers, men like Francis Barrallier, George Caley and George Bass, all of whom lost their way and were forced to return defeated. Only when drought drove the colonists to break out in search of new pastures for their cattle did they succeed in finding a way across. Gregory Blaxland, William Wentworth, William Lawson and their convict servants made it in 1813.

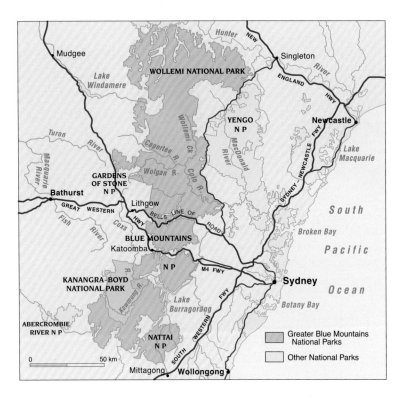

Covering more than 10,000 sq. km, the parks and reserves that protect the Greater Blue Mountains region grew out of a concerted push by bushwalking conservationists from the early 1930s. The first reserve, a 62,000 ha portion of the Blue Mountains National Park (since enlarged to 247,000 ha,) was declared in 1959. Then followed Kanangra-Boyd (1969), Wollemi (1979), Nattai (1991), and Gardens of Stone (1994).

In sinuous embrace (opposite), the Great Western Highway and the railway line snake eastwards through Wentworth Falls township and the lower Blue Mountains towards distant Sydney. Seen from the air, the urban strip that makes up the City of the Blue Mountains appears dwarfed by the immensity of the bush around it. The Devils Wilderness, at top left, confounded the 1804 explorer of the Grose Valley, George Caley, and still presents a formidable challenge to the hardiest bushwalkers.

A road followed quickly, then in the 1860s a railway line. Settlements sprang up along the railway like knots in string, their prodigious growth fuelled in the late 1800s and through most of the 1900s by mass tourism. Today 26 towns and villages make up the City of the Blue Mountains, a 60 km long urban strip bisecting the range along the continuous ridge that Blaxland, Wentworth and Lawson traversed.

The magic of the Blue Mountains is that this city hardly makes a dent in the wildness of the landscape. On either side of it, the bush spreads north and south as far as the eye can see. Here can be found the world's highest density of eucalypt species and 400 different kinds of animal, 40 of them rare or threatened. Here are places never visited by humans.

Developers did eye the bush, but whatever dreams they had of dams, power stations, mines, timber operations and cattle runs generally came to nothing, initially because the terrain proved so formidable but in the end mainly because the bush came to be seen as a valuable asset in itself. From the 1930s, those who had become most familiar with it – the bushwalkers – began campaigning for its protection.

The success of their struggle can be gauged by the mosaic of national parks and reserves that now covers a region generally referred to as the Greater Blue Mountains, spreading from Mittagong in the south to the Hunter and Goulburn rivers in the north. Five national parks lie at the heart of the region – Blue Mountains, Kanangra-Boyd, Nattai, Wollemi and Gardens of Stone – but others have attached themselves to it, including Yengo, Dharug and Goulburn River. They form a huge green crescent abutting Australia's biggest city; an island of primeval landscape in a sea of development.

Four of these parks contain areas of wilderness recognised and protected by the New South Wales Government's *Wilderness Act* 1987. In the late 1980s, a number of community groups began pressing for the Greater Blue Mountains to be placed on the World Heritage List before 2000. The proposal gained political approval in 1997 and was submitted to the UNESCO World Heritage Committee in 1998.

Some 2.3 million people, the equivalent of more than half of Sydney's population, succumb every year to the lure of the mountains, making tourism the region's biggest industry. Visitors are attracted not only to the bush and the peace or adventure it can offer, but also to the urban strip. Indeed, the magic of the mountains is the very amalgam of the faded, though reviving, grandeur of the older towns and their stupendous natural setting.

Artists and writers, along with well-heeled city escapees, have lent some of these settlements a sophisticated air. Art galleries, museums, impressive homes, hotels, motels, guesthouses, resorts, historic villages and European-style gardens that mark the passing of the seasons – all are within cooee of sandstone precipices that tempt rock climbers and abseilers and tracks that can take bushwalkers and mountain-bikers out of the tourist comfort-zone deep into the scented bush. You're never far from the limit of the familiar here.

I've been lured too. I've visited the mountains more times than I can remember, and in the 1980s I lived in the lower Blue Mountains for two unforgettable years. When the opportunity arose to write a book about the region, I could not resist.

This book documents my travels through the Greater Blue Mountains in 1998. I began in the south and worked my way north, moving from wilderness, through the urban strip and back into wilderness. In the bush I travelled on foot and by four-wheel-drive vehicle; in the urban centre I used cars, buses and trains – and my feet. For a good deal of the time I was accompanied by photographer Don Fuchs.

We saw many things and had many adventures, but at no time did I lose my wonder that in Sydney, this teeming and sophisticated city, we have a true wilderness in our backyard.

Kanangra country
Wilderness of the far south

Kanangra Gorge yawns darkly beneath a jagged overhang on Kanangra Walls. This stunning spot has something to offer both the car-based visitor who has time for only a picnic or the self-sufficient adventurer wanting to engage seriously with the landscape. The views are breathtaking and the bushwalking anything from quick and gentle to extended and demanding. The canyoning here is among the best in Australia.

The kookaburra laugh was a giveaway. It was one of the many bird calls reverberating off the walls of the inky gorge in the dawn chorus. I also recognised an eastern whipbird, a black cockatoo and a lyrebird. I wondered why the laugh sounded so odd. Then it struck me: the caller was not a kookaburra at all but a superb lyrebird, icon of Australia's south-eastern forests. This inveterate mimic often issues a stream of other birds' calls interspersed with its own song. And not just bird calls; it has been heard imitating everything from cats to chainsaws – even a camera's motor-drive.

"Liar-bird," I muttered.

The cloud of my breath hung briefly before me, gilded by the horizontal rays of the rising sun. I was sitting with my legs dangling over the edge of a cliff. Below me a gorge still lay in its pool of cold darkness. It was 500 m to the bottom of the gorge, though the cliff fell vertically for less than a third of that before meeting scrub-cloaked scree. From the darkness came the whisper of a creek.

I was looking down from Kanangra Walls in the heart of Kanangra-Boyd National Park (NP). I'd driven here with Don Fuchs before sunrise. As a bright line spread across the eastern horizon,

we'd sat down on the rim of the still-invisible gorge to watch the show.

As the first rocks began to glow gold on Thurat Walls and Thurat Spires opposite me, the black depths turned a luminous magenta. To the northeast, in the deep gullies below Mount Cloudmaker and towards Narrow Neck, near the town of Katoomba, 35 km away, mist lay in soft pools. I imagined some of the region's original inhabitants, the Gundungurra people, peering into similar valleys and watching pale-skinned invaders struggling against all logic up the creek lines from the east. Didn't they know that the way across was via the ridges? They did (contrary to some historians' claims), but the first European explorers to penetrate this part of the world had great trouble finding ridges that led anywhere.

By 7.20 the cliffs around me were glowing a rich gold and the gorge had turned from magenta to dark green. Waterfalls, swollen by recent rain, hung like silver streamers from precipices. At that moment I understood why people flocked to stare into these magnificent depths. Here were elements of everything that characterises the Blue Mountains region as a whole: formidable sandstone cliffs; a forbidding gorge darkened by dense vegetation;

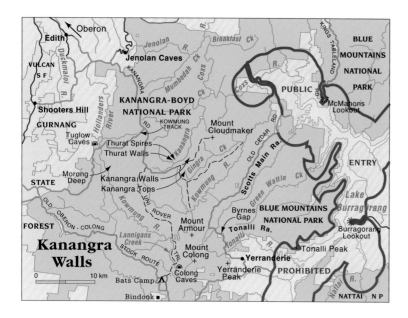

Kanangra
Walls

Bushwalkers head west along the edge of Kanangra Walls towards the car park at the head of Kanangra Gorge. The plateau behind the walls, known as Kanangra Tops, is covered in heath, low, shrubby vegetation with few tall trees. One of the most abundant plants in this windswept spot is the heath banksia, which flowers in winter and provides food for several species of honeyeater. Thomas Seymour is thought to have been the first European to see the walls. He stumbled upon Kanangra Tops while looking for lost cattle in 1864. He is quoted as saying: "I climbed the Walls, and on the top found a chair-shaped rock, and resting there I viewed one of the greatest sights of my life."

views over an ocean of undulating blue-green wilderness to awe the visitor and beckon the adventurous; a combination of unique vegetation seen nowhere else on this planet; evidence of Aboriginal occupation nearby; and everywhere the signs of the European occupation that began two centuries ago.

With the sun now high in the sky, Don and I took the Plateau Walk along the clifftop to the car park. At one rise, I stopped to admire the view beyond Kanangra Tops to the south. Dominating a densely pleated landscape of eucalypt forest, the basalt-capped summit of Mount Colong rose to 1047 m in the distance. It was close to Colong Caves, our next destination, and though it was only 17 km away as the crow flies, we would have to make a long detour to reach the area.

As I walked, I marvelled at the tenacity of the wind-stunted heath shrubs. With small, hard leaves that resist water loss and shallow but stubborn roots, they cling to the plateau, enduring everything the Australian climate can hurl at them, from searing drought to biting frost and roaring gales. I had an uncontrollable urge to congratulate them on their hardiness.

I'D PICKED KANANGRA WALLS as the starting point of our journey because it lay close to the southern extremity of the whole Blue Mountains complex. I intended to explore from south to north, roughly following the historical progression of the area's transformation from bushland ripe for exploitation to a potential World Heritage property. For it was from the wrangling over this region that the push to conserve the Blue Mountains came to involve a broad spectrum of the NSW public.

From Kanangra we drove back along the Jenolan road for 15 minutes before turning south-west onto the Kowmung Track, which changed rapidly from family-sedan-negotiable to decidedly 4WD-only, with startlingly steep grades and sharp turns on the edges of sheer drops. A last eye-bulging descent brought us to the gravelly banks of the tea-coloured Kowmung River.

I'd heard much about this river. It flows through Kanangra-Boyd NP towards its junction with the Coxs River near Lake Burragorang, the vast artificial reservoir on the eastern side of the Blue Mountains NP. Variously described as "pristine", or the "last wild river", the Kowmung seemed a modest watercourse here at this crossing in its upper reaches, about 6 m wide, shallow and slow. Upstream, I knew, lay Tuglow Caves, high in a limestone bluff. Among several small caves is a deep main cave that requires experience, caving gear and a National Parks and Wildlife Service (NPWS) permit to explore. Downstream, the Kowmung dives into Morong Deep, where it thunders from rock ledges into deep pools on its way to the Upper Kowmung Gorge.

The climb on the other side of the river was as steep as the descent. Soon we were on a ridgetop where the woodland was thin and dry. Then, most unexpectedly, we found ourselves driving with eucalypt woodland on our left and pines on our right, a weird juxtaposition of native and introduced trees. The pines were in Gurnang State Forest, which the Kowmung Track separates from the national park.

TIME AND WATER

The Blue Mountains are the remains of a plateau that has been mostly washed away by rivers and creeks.

The rock strata that make up the plateau were laid down as layers of sand, silt and the remains of plants in a vast coastal inlet, known as the Sydney Basin, about 250 million years ago. This bay stretched from present-day Sydney to Rockhampton in Queensland.

Rivers flowing into the bay eventually filled it with sediment, forcing the sea back and creating deltas and swamps. Thereafter rivers continued to deposit sand on these deltas and swamps.

Between 90 and 35 million years ago, a geological upheaval raised the sediment-filled bay to create a plateau that sloped gently downward from west to east. It was a relatively slow process, allowing the existing rivers and creeks to cut down through the sedimentary layers, now compressed and turned mainly to sandstone, and create the dramatic landscape that is the Blue Mountains.

Not all the prominent features of the Blue Mountains are purely sedimentary. Some may have once stood as islands of older quartzite in the sedimentary basin. Others are capped by hard basalt that was spewed out as lava during volcanic eruptions about 15 million years ago. The remains of volcanoes active during the geological upheaval between 90 and 35 million years ago can be seen as circular depressions or amphitheatres throughout the region.

The geological history of the Blue Mountains shows the enormous impact that time and even relatively small river systems can have on a landscape.

Carrying a heavy load of silt, rivers and creeks cut down through the sandstone of the plateau that was formed about 90–35 million years ago. Initially the erosion carved steep-sided gorges, but as the water washed less-stable shale from under their slopes, it created overhangs that in time collapsed. This resulted in the sheer cliffs that today rise from scree slopes, the debris of their collapse.

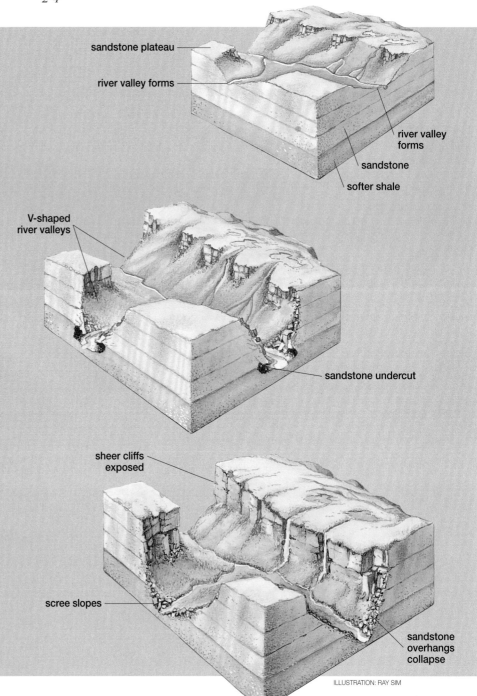

sandstone plateau

river valley forms

river valley forms

sandstone

softer shale

V-shaped river valleys

sandstone undercut

sheer cliffs exposed

scree slopes

sandstone overhangs collapse

ILLUSTRATION: RAY SIM

Five kilometres further on we turned left onto the road that follows the old Oberon–Colong Stock Route south-east through the park. Just before reaching a grazing property named *Bindook*, we turned off the track towards Bats Camp, a camping ground where NPWS ranger Vanessa Richardson was waiting for us.

Shouldering our packs, we began the 3 km walk to Colong Caves through a sparse woodland of mountain gums, ribbon gums and acacias. Beyond what is a closed 4WD track, we began one of the steepest descents I have ever negotiated on two feet, my mind fixating on the next day, when we'd have to climb out by the same route.

As we plunged into what seemed a bottomless ravine, we could make out through the treetops (at eye level, thanks to the gradient) a rough-hewn limestone cliff. This

Dawn gilds the head of Kanangra Walls. Soon the sun's rays will melt the lake of mist that sits in the appropriately named Misty Gully, above Kanangra Falls. Just as water has shaped the landscape through the aeons, so it continues to dominate the area's environment today. The gently undulating Boyd Plateau, stretching to the horizon beyond the mist, is a maze of creeks and rivers that flow through swamps, eucalypt forest and heath. This is rich habitat for an assortment of wildlife including eastern grey kangaroos, swamp wallabies and wombats.

THE ABORIGINAL VIEW

In the Dreamtime, Guranggatch – part fish, part reptile – who lived in the Wollondilly River, was attacked by Mirragan the tiger cat (spotted-tailed quoll), a skilful fisherman. Although large and powerful, Guranggatch fled from Mirragan, managing to outwit him by digging out the Wollondilly valley as he went and causing the water to flow after him. When the furious chase was over, Guranggatch had carved the valleys of the Wollondilly and Coxs rivers and many of their tributaries.

In inky tendrils, the Nattai River weaves through its dusk-darkened valley towards Lake Burragorang, which covers its former confluence with the Wollondilly River. The Bluff dominates the skyline.

With cloud-topped Thurat Walls (above) in the middle distance, Greg Kerr contemplates the descent he is about to make into a canyon at Kanangra Gorge. On the 1–6 canyon-grading scale of difficulty, this one stands at 6 and has been described as "awesome" by experienced canyoners and "very hazardous" by the NPWS. It includes three long abseils beside a 150 m high waterfall and should not be attempted without expert guidance.

Ashley Kaar (opposite left) prepares to make a 55 m abseil into Kanangra Gorge. Below the main drop on this route, shorter descents lead to the bottom of the gorge. Greg Kerr (opposite right) halfway down one of the waterfalls in Kanangra Gorge.

NPWS ranger Vanessa Richardson and author Peter Meredith set off from Bats Camp on the 3 km track to Lannigans Creek and Colong Caves. Just off the Oberon–Colong Stock Route, Bats Camp is a starting point and destination for numerous bushwalks. One of the most popular walking tracks in Kanangra-Boyd National Park is the Uni Rover Trail, which takes walkers from Bats Camp down to the Kowmung River and up to the Kanangra-Boyd Plateau.

is the largest of several limestone outcrops in the southern Blue Mountains, most of them renowned for their caves. Apart from the outcrop at Colong, they include those at Jenolan, Tuglow and Wombeyan. Less well known these days is the Mount Armour outcrop, some 5 km north-east of Colong, though from the late 1960s into the early '70s it was making headlines.

The Colong cave system, with a total passage length of about 6 km on three levels, has two entrances, both above Caves Creek, a tributary of Lannigans Creek, to which we were descending. Edward Lannigan, a local landholder and cattle-duffer, is popularly said to have discovered the caves in 1896, though this would make him 95 years old at the time. Government geologist Oliver Trickett surveyed them in 1899 and, noting their fine crystal formations, recommended they be officially protected. The State Government duly created a reserve around them that year. In the early 1900s, miners and their families made regular sightseeing trips to the caves from Yerranderie, a nearby silver-mining settlement.

The formations Trickett had documented had mostly been souvenired by the time legendary bushwalker Myles Dunphy, on the first of his many visits to the area, arrived there with walking companion Bert Gallop on 8 October 1913. They found two miners, Lucien Fattorini and Hardy Smith, blasting their way through the caves with dynamite. Myles and Bert followed the men into a cave that one of their explosions had revealed. Myles reported seeing floor formations "like embroidered amber pancakes, of a composition not unlike caked brown sugar" and predicted that visitors would soon trample or steal most of the structures. He was right. To guard against further vandalism, the NPWS now requires visitors to have permits.

Finding the caves was not easy. At the bottom of our 200 m descent, we lost our bearings in the dense rainforest on Lannigans Creek. It was extraordinarily rugged in that ravine, almost exactly as Myles had described it 85 years previously: "… choked with broken white marble, limestone, dead timber and nettles … an awfully wild place …"

During his many subsequent bushwalks through the southern Blue Mountains, some of them covering hundreds of kilometres, Myles never ceased to be moved by the beauty of the landscape. Together with other members of the Mountain Trails Club, which he and Bert formed in 1914, they penetrated regions never before visited by Europeans. By the early 1930s, walkers from Sydney were claiming Kanangra country as their own. Myles, a lecturer in architecture, an artist and calligrapher, meticulously mapped the area and named most of its features, convinced that good mapping and nomenclature were a means of gaining converts to the bushwalking–conservation cause.

Adventurous visitors exploring damp sandstone gullies may come across the native fuchsia heath (below left), a small shrub that prefers moist ledges on sheltered cliff faces. It is restricted to the upper Blue Mountains. Campers at the Boyd River camping area are bound to catch sight of the numerous eastern grey kangaroos (below) that graze on the lush swampy flats along the Boyd (also called Morong Creek). The camping area is on the southern extremity of the Boyd Plateau, which reaches its maximum height at 1334 m high Mt Emperor. The plateau is covered in subalpine vegetation that includes heath, snow gums, rainforest, mossy swamps and snowgrass.

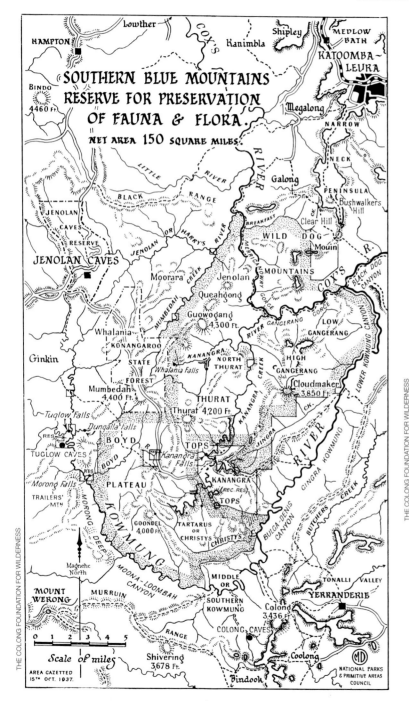

Bushwalking conservationist Myles Dunphy, left, then an architecture student, and mate Bert Gallop, an art student, at Jenolan Caves in 1912. The pair were sightseeing during a 230 km bushwalk. Walkers commonly carried guns in those days, mainly to shoot rabbits for the pot. Myles' extended walks in the Blue Mountains enabled him to produce meticulous maps (left), which be used as potent weapons in his campaigns to conserve the area. One of the spots he regularly visited on his walks was Yerranderie, a former silver-mining township east of Colong Caves. The settlement is overlooked by Bartlett Head (opposite).

Undoubtedly influenced by park-creation moves overseas, Myles drew up a plan for a Blue Mountains National Park. Covering 4662 sq. km and stretching more than 140 km from north to south, it was the largest scheme of its kind ever proposed in Australia. At its heart would lie a "primitive area", a term used officially in the USA after 1929 to mean a roadless wilderness accessible only to adventurers on foot. It was split into three divisions – Southern, Central and Northern.

To promote this and other park proposals, several walking groups formed the National Parks and Primitive Areas Council (NPPAC), with Myles as its secretary. Myles and the NPPAC embarked on a massive campaign to publicise the Blue Mountains park proposal, culminating in a four-page supplement to the *Katoomba Daily* in 1934. However, 26 years elapsed before a segment of Myles's park was officially reserved in 1959 as the 62,000-hectare Blue Mountains NP. From this modest start grew the conglomerate of five parks that protects the region today.

The more impressive of the two entrances to Colong Caves is the Grand Arch, reached by a short scramble up from Caves Creek. Here we sat and recovered from our workout. We were sitting on a smooth mound of limestone. The arch soared above us, stalactites hanging like daggers from its roof amid a spray of cave spiders' webs. Below and behind us stood two stunted stalagmites, one shorter than the other, aptly called the Mother and Child. We were, Vanessa said, three of about 400 people who visit Colong Caves annually.

"You have to be well prepared and have some experience and fitness to explore this system," she said.

Along with the spiders, Vanessa said, the caves were home to eastern horseshoe and common bent-wing bats, sooty owls and a species of cave cricket. To Vanessa, the caves' importance lay not only in their natural values but also in their historical association with the battle that erupted when it became known that a cement company was planning to mine 50 million tonnes of limestone at Mount Armour. Although the mining would take place in only a small part of the Colong Caves Reserve and would not damage the caves themselves, it would scar an area clearly visible from Kanangra Walls, and other caves closer to Mount Armour would be damaged.

The outcry over this proposal led in 1968 to the formation of the Colong Committee (renamed the Colong Foundation for Wilderness in 1985) by Myles's son Milo. The committee galvanised public opinion and, aided by 50 conservation-minded organisations, fought a bitter battle against the State Government and the cement company. Overwhelmed, the Government revoked the mining leases in 1974 and added the area to Kanangra-Boyd NP, another segment of Myles's proposed park, declared in 1969.

The Colong campaign was the beginning of a new era in conservation. For the first time in Australia, the preservation of nature became a public issue, uniting people from all sectors of society.

Dense temperate rainforest (opposite) surrounds the clearing where Peter Meredith and photographer Don Fuchs camped at the junction of Lannigans and Caves creeks, near Colong Caves. It turned out to be 20 m from where Myles Dunphy and Bert Gallop had camped in 1912. Vanessa Richardson (left) leads the way into the Grand Arch, one of two entrances to Colong Caves. Though lacking impressive formations, the Colong system's 6 km of passages are popular with cavers – who require a permit from NPWS. Bracket fungi (below) decorate one of the many rotting logs that lie across Lannigans Creek. Like most of the creeks flowing into the Kowmung River, Lannigans is infested with nettles, both native and exotic.

"These caves are a conservation icon," Vanessa said. "It's where the modern conservation movement was born. Without the Colong campaign we wouldn't have the national parks we have today."

After Vanessa had left, Don and I made tentative explorations of part of the cave system. We came to a point where a tunnel widened in front of us and sloped downward into nothingness. I threw a small rock. It took what seemed ages to hit the bottom. With no proper caving gear, and with our torches starting to dim, we turned back.

Deciding that the NPWS-approved Caves Creek camping area was too dark and cold, we pitched our tents further downstream on a grassy patch at the junction of Caves and Lannigans creeks. I'd heard stories about the ghost of a climber who had been killed when he fell from the limestone bluff above us in 1964 and had reportedly appeared to several campers at this spot since then. We saw no ghost, but the presence of Fattorini, Smith, Myles and Bert was palpable. Next morning, consulting a photocopy of Myles's sketch-map of the creek junction, I discovered we had unknowingly camped on the very spot chosen by Fattorini and Smith in 1913. Myles and Bert had camped 20 m away.

HAD WE BEEN DESTINED TO SEE A GHOST, it could just as likely have been that of a horse. In 1970 Val Lang, at the time running *Bindook* with her husband, Neville, climbed down the steep track to Lannigans Creek in search of a stray horse. She found it had fallen to its death. When Don and I visited Val in her homestead a short drive from Bats Camp, she said: "That was the only time I've been down to the caves. I thought, Gosh, I don't need this hill – it's a shocker!"

The old homestead on BINDOOK has been partly restored and (sometimes in bad weather) cattle farmer Val Lang lets bushwalkers use it as they pass through her land on their way to or from Bindook Falls and Bindook Gorge, a popular canyoning site. More than 65 years old, the building stands above Bindook Creek, which rises in Bent Hook Swamp, 2–3 km south of Colong Caves.

A trim grandmotherly figure with large tinted spectacles and a ruddy complexion, Val welcomed us into her warm kitchen and chatted to us in her shy, quiet way while making pikelets for expected guests. Could this really be the hard-bitten farmer I'd heard about, the woman who'd reputedly been managing two cattle properties since Neville had died 10 years ago?

Beyond the kitchen window, green paddocks rolled down to Bindook Creek, which rises at Bent Hook Swamp, close to Bats Camp. The ridges above the paddocks were covered with the bush of the Blue Mountains NP. Val grew up on a farm in the district, marrying Neville, who was helping his father run *Bindook*, in 1953. Neville took over the farm at the age of 21 when his father died.

After Neville's death, Val managed *Bindook* with the help of her brother, Phil Scarlett. She taught her son and two daughters at home until they could go to boarding school. One daughter was now a paraplegic in a nursing home and her son had died at the age of 39 from a virus a year before I met her. Despite this she was carrying on cheerfully, breeding cattle on her 800 ha at *Bindook* and at her other property south-west of Oberon.

At *Bindook* she was finding herself increasingly isolated. Many former farming neighbours had been displaced by the creation of Lake Burragorang (together with its extensive exclusion zone) in the 1950s, the spread of the national parks system on three sides of *Bindook* and increasingly difficult economic conditions.

Val had a thing or two to say about the national park around her: "When you're surrounded by bush, it's extremely difficult to keep the vermin out. You're much better off with farming neighbours because most look after their weeds and vermin and you work together."

Apart from the "vermin" (a term Val used for both native and exotic animals), her other main concern was about the fire risk posed by the park. In December 1997, lightning strikes started fires in the Bindook Highlands, immediately to *Bindook's* east. For six weeks firefighters struggled to prevent the eastward and northward march of the fire front. Eventually, after scarring 75,000 ha of the Blue Mountains and Nattai national parks, the fire burnt itself out.

Expecting guests, Val Lang (above right) whips up some tasty pikelets in the kitchen of her homestead on her 800 ha cattle property, BINDOOK. One of the hazards of living surrounded by bush, Val claims, is the risk that fire will break out in inaccessible areas – as it did in 1997 in the nearby Bindook Highlands – and spread to farming country. Scorched trees (right) are testimony to the intensity of bushfires in the Blue Mountains National Park.

IAN BROWN

Bartlett Head soars above Slippery Norris's cottage (right), one of the buildings in Yerranderie township. During its heyday in the early 1900s, when output from its 27 silver mines was at its peak, Yerranderie consisted of four separate centres – including Private Town and Government Town – with a total population of 2000. Lovingly restored and maintained by its owner, architect Val Lhuede, 76, Private Town now attracts bushwalkers and adventurous motorists. Visitors can either camp or stay in some of the settlement's historic buildings, including the home of former Gallipoli veteran Frank "Slippery" Norris. Mrs Barnes's Boarding House (below), a slab and corrugated-iron home, was the first building to be put up in this part of Yerranderie and has been preserved in its original state, complete with many artefacts, furnishings and fittings of the period.

Val Lhuede (left) cuddles Kiara Hopwood, aged 3, daughter of John and Lyn Hopwood, who worked as part-time caretakers at Yerranderie. Though she lives in Sydney, Val flies to the township on most weekends. The shop in the background, run by Sam Meldrum for more than 15 years from 1912, now serves as Yerranderie's souvenir shop. John Kirkby (below), current part-time caretaker at Yerranderie, holds Harry, an orphaned wombat that had made itself at home in the historic township. When John, 53, and wife Rosemary aren't looking after Yerranderie, they run a tour business in the Southern Highlands. John also advises Val on financial affairs.

TO THE NORTH-EAST OF *BINDOOK*, about 15 km as the crow flies but nearly twice that distance by road, another Val has made her mark on the landscape. She, too, has property surrounded by public land, but it's not a farm she owns – it's a township.

Born in 1923, Val Lhuede is the daughter of Aubin Lhuede, a real-estate agent and would-be silver-miner. Aubin was a colleague of real-estate magnate Leslie Joseph Hooker, who in 1947 needed a liquor licence for the first of a chain of hotels. At the time a portion of Yerranderie, the mining settlement not far from Colong Caves, was on the market. The parcel covered what was called Private Town, one of four separate centres in the settlement. Owned by Harold Clyde Manning, it included the Silver Mine Hotel, a post office, a Bank of New South Wales branch, a boarding house, a general store, a tailor's shop, a bakery, the cottages of miners – including Gallipoli veteran Frank "Slippery" Norris – and about a dozen silver mines. Hooker bought the parcel, kept the hotel's licence and sold the land, buildings and mining leases to a company set up by Aubin Lhuede and some partners.

"Yerranderie was still a township then, though the mines had folded during the Depression," Val told me when I visited her in her Sydney home. "Dad found that the silver leases were still current, so he had the idea to get some of the mines going again."

HARD-WON RICHES

Mining began seriously at Yerranderie in 1898, when John Bartlett established Colon Peaks (later Bartlett's) Mine. Other mines followed, though only 4–5 of the 27 eventually opened had any success. First-class silver-lead ore was carted by horse teams 65 km through the Burragorang Valley to Camden until motor transport was introduced in 1921. Despite strong lobbying, proposals for a railway link came to nothing. The second-class ore, 80 per cent of the orebody, was never treated because its bulk made it uneconomic to transport.

Output from the mines rose rapidly in the early 1900s, peaking in 1908–12. In 1908, 23 tonnes of silver and 1892 tonnes of lead were produced from 7402 tonnes of ore. Yerranderie township prospered and in its heyday had a population of 2000. As well as the buildings still standing today, there was a school for 65 children, a police station and courthouse, a butchery and a dance hall.

A crippling 10-month strike in 1925, combined with falling metal prices and the increasing difficulty of winning the ore, spelt doom for Yerranderie. By 1930 production was down to 2.2 tonnes of silver and 187 tonnes of lead from 448 tonnes of ore. After ceasing for three years, production revived briefly before the last of the mines closed in 1936.

In 39 years Yerranderie produced 340 tonnes of silver, 28,000 tonnes of lead, 623 kg of gold and small amounts of zinc and copper from 123,735 tonnes of ore.

Miners (above right) take a break outside the Hell Hole Mine at Yerranderie. Miners worked a six-day, 44-hour week, for which they earned the equivalent of $180. It was hard, dangerous work in dusty conditions that encouraged silicosis, a lung disease. Miners were issued with three candles for each shift, though supervisors were allowed carbide lamps. The Silver Peak Mine (right), was the only mine at Yerranderie with a vertical main shaft. The mine's workings reached a depth of 300 m.

COURTESY: VALERIE LHUEDE COLLECTION

After the war, when she was in her early 20s and starting an architectural career, Val visited Yerranderie regularly and would go horseriding and bushwalking around the township. Aubin's silver-mining venture came to nothing, but convinced that Yerranderie had potential as an educational tourist destination, she gradually bought out her father's partners and also most of Government Town, another part of Yerranderie. She now owns 468 ha of the settlement; the rest is divided between Sydney Water and private owners.

Her plans for the township relied on access from the east. A road had existed before Lake Burragorang was created, and Val was told a new one would be built after the old one was submerged. A new road was built, but because it traverses the prohibited area around the lake, it has remained closed to the public except for occasional NPWS-guided tours to Yerranderie. When land was resumed for the lake, landowners were compensated for the loss of access. Sydney Water and the NPWS, which jointly manage the lake – the major source of Sydney's drinking water – and its catchment, say excluding the public from around the lake is essential for keeping its water pure.

"So Yerranderie was isolated," Val said.

That's no exaggeration. The township is entirely surrounded by the Blue Mountains NP, Lake Burragorang and the Nattai reserves system. Though it's less than 100 km from Sydney's centre, reaching it takes 4–5 hours' driving on some very rough roads, most of which are impassable after rain.

Undaunted, Val set about restoring the derelict township with the help of caretakers she employed. It was a true labour of love, since she knew that without an eastern road there would never be enough visitors to make the place pay. "I don't count the cost," Val said. "My dream would come true if we could have enough people to sustain Yerranderie, but at the moment it is funded largely by me. I do try hard to make it pay."

Bushwalkers, four-wheel-drivers and determined visitors in tough two-wheel-drive vehicles are her main clientele. At weekends, Val flies in from Sydney (where she lives and works). Now 76, she enjoys yarning with visitors who, like me, come away impressed by her enthusiasm for the piece of Australian heritage she feels privileged to own.

Don and I arrived on a brilliant afternoon, when Yerranderie's lawns glowed a vivid green and the restored buildings sparkled. Over the peaceful scene towered flat-topped Bartlett Head, a bluff on the eastern arm of 873 m high Yerranderie Peak. It was plain to see that Val was just managing to keep ahead of nature's advance guard. All around, the bush pressed in. Only the general store remained to be refurbished, but the job would have to be started soon if termites weren't going to consume the entire building.

We were greeted by grey-bearded John Kirkby, 53, one of Val's two caretakers. When he's not on duty at Yerranderie, John and his wife Rosemary run a 4WD and

Tailings surround the derelict Silver Peak Mine, one of only a handful around Yerranderie that eventually proved profitable. A 10-minute walk from the township, the mine is just outside Val's land in the Blue Mountains National Park. The opening to the main shaft is fenced off but a walkway above it enables visitors to peer into its depths.

bushwalking tour business in NSW's Southern Highlands. He spoke admiringly of Val and her commitment to Yerranderie, echoing her remarks about limited access.

"But it's nice that you can be so close to Sydney and still have this isolation," he added. "There can't be too many places in the world like it."

Next morning, Don and I rose before dawn to make the 200 m ascent of Bartlett Head. By the time we reached the summit, sunlight had begun to flood into the valley below and smoke was rising from fires in Yerranderie's camping ground. The township seemed lost in a sea of green, its derelict mines vanishing under the encroaching bush. I found it hard to believe that 2000 people once lived and worked here.

In all directions lay an extraordinarily wild landscape. To the south-east the low hills of Nattai NP rose and dipped like grey-green ocean swells. Straddling the Nattai River and created a park in 1991, this was among the areas that Myles Dunphy proposed for reservation in his 1932 Blue Mountains National Park plan. Nattai covers 47,000 ha and has at its core a wilderness of 29,882 ha that protects one of the few large areas of almost undisturbed bushland left in NSW.

To the north, beyond the Tonalli River valley, marched the serrations and walls of the Tonalli Range. At the range's eastern extension, Tonalli Peak rose above the mist blanketing Lake Burragorang. In 1802, exploring on orders from NSW Governor Philip Gidley King, Francis Barrallier had decided to keep heading due west, whatever the obstacles. On his first attempt to travel up the Tonalli, he tried unsuccessfully to climb the peak to scout the land ahead. On his second foray, he halted his men near Byrnes Gap, a pass through the western end of the Tonalli Range, and climbed a rise for a view westward. Beyond Scotts Main Range he would have seen Kanangra Tops, which I was looking at now. Unable to discern the gorge of the Kowmung River, he was deceived into thinking a relatively flat plain lay between him and the distant tops.

It was a crucial mistake but one easily made in this labyrinthine terrain.

Historic graffiti, carved by early visitors to Bartlett Head – a popular climb since the early 1890s – mark a rock 200 m above Yerranderie. The climb is for the moderately fit and energetic and takes about an hour. In this dawn shot, the remains of the Silver Peak Mine, as well as Yerranderie's buildings and the lawn of its camping area, still lie in shadow. Through the valley beyond the village runs the Tonalli River, which flows into Lake Burragorang. In the distance, behind Byrnes Gap, lie Scotts Main Range and Kanangra Tops.

TRAVEL ADVICE

While some of the places mentioned in this and later chapters are within reach of the car-based tourist, others are out of bounds to motor vehicles. Always inquire in advance where you can drive and what state the tracks are in – some are closed in wet weather. Remember that the Blue Mountains experiences all kinds of weather, from snowstorms to heatwaves. Come well prepared. Be aware that bushfires are a constant danger.

For information on tracks in Kanangra-Boyd and Blue Mountains national parks, as well as on ranger-guided walks and other activities, contact the NPWS headquarters at the Heritage Centre, Govetts Leap Rd, Blackheath, 2785, ☎ 02 4787 8877, <www.npws.nsw.gov.au>. You need NPWS permits to explore Tuglow and Colong caves. Try the Blue Mountains Speleological Club, PO Box 37, Glenbrook 2773.

Yerranderie can be reached from Sydney via the Great Western Highway or Bells Line of Road and Oberon. From Oberon you can drive via Shooters Hill or detour via Jenolan Caves and the Kowmung Track (4WD needed); in both cases you reach Yerranderie on The Oberon–Colong Stock Route. A southern route takes you via Mittagong and Wombeyan Caves (4WD needed). Large buses, small cars and cars pulling trailers or caravans should not attempt the journey. Rain can make all access roads impassable.

If you don't want to drive, you can fly from Camden, in Sydney's south-west. The flight to the Yerranderie airstrip takes 20 minutes. Contact Curtis Air ☎ 02 4655 6789. Yerranderie offers several types of accommodation. ☎ 02 9955 8063, 02 9929 8350 or 02 4659 6165.

Tin-can alley. A distinctive sign directs visitors to Wonga Mine, formerly among Yerranderie's richest. It is a 25-minute walk due north of the village. Fossickers may find specimens of silver in its mullock heaps.

A lake and a river

Lake Burragorang and the Kowmung River

The skeletons of dead river oaks on the banks of Coxs River glow eerily in the light cast by an approaching thunderstorm. The Coxs rises on the Great Dividing Range in Ben Bullen State Forest, north of Lithgow, and is drained to supply water for two power stations before it flows south and east to Lake Burragorang. Its lower reaches were first settled in the 1820s.

Myles Dunphy likened Byrnes Gap to "gigantic portals to another world". And on seeing what lay beyond, he wrote: "Believe me, we Australians have no need to visit other countries until we have seen our own scenery first."

Don and I drove out of Yerranderie, through Byrnes Gap and onto Scotts Main Range. Because it's in wilderness, the track along the top of the range is normally barred by a locked gate. In addition, access is through private land. However, we had been given official permission to explore by vehicle.

The NPWS defines a wilderness as "a large natural area where plant and animal communities are relatively undisturbed and which provides opportunities for solitude and self-reliant recreation". In other words, no motorised vehicles of any kind, and no horses. The *Wilderness Act 1987* provides for the protection of wilderness and allows any person or organisation to propose areas for declaration as such. Although the declared wilderness areas in the Blue Mountains national parks are crossed by tracks in many places, these have been closed to vehicles and horseriders. They remain open to bushwalkers and mountain-bikers and are used by the authorities for emergencies such as fires.

The bush on Scotts Main Range had been badly seared by the 1997–98 fires. Nevertheless, much of the canopy remained, and everywhere the bright sprays of young spikes emerged from the charred trunks of the grass trees.

This wilderness once echoed to the thunder of hooves. From the 1860s, Scotts Main Range road was a well-trodden cattle track and a section of it, built in 1907 and called the Cedar Road, was also used by cedar-getters working down on the Kowmung and its tributaries. As though to recall those horse-dependent times, a mob of seven brumbies burst onto the track and began galloping ahead of us. It was my first encounter with introduced animals inside the park. My second came moments later when a fox slunk off the road at our approach. The exotic animals and the possible impacts of cattle and timber operations set me wondering how much use and abuse at the hands of humans a landscape could undergo before it could no longer be classed as wilderness; it was a question that would worry me for much of my time in the Blue Mountains.

We dropped off the end of the range from Sugarloaf Hill into the prohibited area around Lake Burragorang. Minutes later the lake's north-

Beauty out of bounds. A magical landscape of fiords and bush spreads from near McMahons Lookout, on the southern tip of Kings Tableland, which overlooks the north-western arm of Lake Burragorang. This 7500 ha reservoir is nearly 30 per cent bigger than Sydney Harbour and provides 80 per cent of Sydney's drinking water. It is a no-go area for the public, as is an area of land of varying width around it.

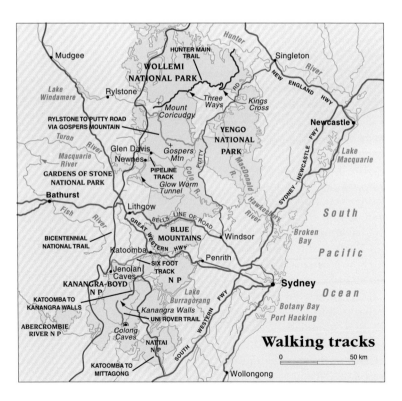

Walking tracks

0   50 km

western arm came into view. It was, as I'd heard tell, a very beautiful body of water. Its mirror surface reflected the towering crags and bushy slopes around it, the reflection punctured by scores of black swans. Being only 60 per cent full, the lake was rimmed by a sandy shoreline that river oaks, gums and grass were fast reclaiming.

When we stopped the engine, thick silence enveloped us. I was in one of the most restricted areas in Australia, and, although I'd been able to enter it remarkably easily, for nearly all other Australians this mesmerising place is out of bounds. The lake's isolation was therefore as artificial as the lake itself. As I stood there, neither seemed real. It was a most uncanny sensation.

I was to have an even more uncanny experience soon afterwards. I was sitting talking to Mark Mallitt, a production officer with Sydney Water, in a speedboat wallowing quietly in the middle of the lake. We'd come from Warragamba Dam and had stopped opposite Junction Point, where the three arms of the star-shaped lake meet. Bellbirds tinkled on the shore.

We were directly above what used to be called Cox Junction, the confluence of the Coxs and Wollondilly rivers. Two churches once stood on either side of the vanished confluence, one Catholic and one Anglican. Like many other buildings in the

A Sydney Water speedboat carves a white slash through Lake Burragorang beneath the crags of Wanganderry Walls. The lake holds 2 million megalitres, compared with Sydney Harbour's half-million. Excluding the public from the lake and the surrounding land helps maintain water quality and is relatively easy. But keeping out animals, such as this eastern grey kangaroo (inset), is almost impossible. Animals, both feral and native, are a source of pollution and erosion.

Lake Burragorang is held in check by Warragamba Dam in Warragamba Gorge. Work started on the dam in 1948 over the protests of residents of the Burragorang Valley, a bountiful region that had supported Gundungurra people for thousands of years and, from the 1820s, was developed as farmland, in the main by emancipated convicts. Land resumptions started in 1950, after which the valley filled gradually. The dam, 351 m long, 142 m high and comprising 3 million tonnes of concrete – the largest concrete dam in Australia – was complete, and the reservoir full, by 1960. Relics of the drowned community lie beneath the water and occasionally appear when the dam is low. Near this tree stump (below) are the concrete remains of a cheese factory. The lake's quiet reaches teem with waterbirds, like these black swans (opposite) dwarfed by the sandstone cliffs of Kedumba Walls, on Pearces Mountain.

valley, the Anglican church was dismantled and removed before the lake rose, but the Catholic church was left standing. If you were to dive down there, you might see its remains. You might also make out the outline of the road coming up from the south on its way to Wentworth Falls, near Katoomba. You might see where a school once stood, a convent hall, a mission building and some of the valley's dozen guesthouses. You might meet the ghosts of the mainly Irish settlers, the O'Reillys, Flynns, Quigs, Fitzpatricks and McMahons, who made the Wollondilly and Coxs valleys their own earthly paradise, or of the tourists who used to come from Sydney in the first half of the 1900s. You might also sense the presence of the Gundungurra people, who lived in this bountiful place among the spirits of their ancestors for 20,000 years or more.

When Barrallier traversed the southern end of the Burragorang (a collective name for the Coxs and Wollondilly valleys) in 1802, he encountered a stable Gundungurra community. Graziers, moving into the Burragorang from the mid-1820s, soon displaced them, and by 1900 the Gundungurra were living in two small reserves beside the Wollondilly. The irony is that today the relics of Gundungurra and white settler alike lie lost beneath the lake.

Mark told me his job's focus was water quality. He outlined the various potential threats to the purity of the lake's water, including the sewage effluent and farm runoff entering via the Coxs, Wollondilly and Nattai rivers. These were in such low concentrations in the water that, for all intents and purposes, it was pure where we were sitting, he said. Heavy metals leaching from Yerranderie's old silver mines remained a localised problem confined to the lake's southern end.

Wildlife also had an impact on water quality, Mark pointed out. Some animals broke up the soil surface in the catchment. Horses and cattle did it with their hooves; pigs did it when rooting for food, and wombats when digging their burrows. Rainwater then washed the loosened soil, together with animal droppings, into watercourses and thence into the lake. Humans also caused erosion – with forestry operations higher in the catchment, roadbuilding and driving on unsealed tracks. Hunters and campers illegally driving in the prohibited zone also contributed.

This brought us to the contentious question of whether the prohibited zone might be opened up to recreational users such as four-wheel-drivers, campers and horseriders. The NPWS, Sydney Water and some environmental groups had vigorously opposed any such move and, after lengthy consultations, the State Government had retained the prohibition.

"The restriction is necessary to maintain a stable environment and ensure water quality," Mark said. "If you allowed the various users in, you wouldn't be able to guarantee that quality."

(As though to emphasise the vulnerability of that quality, 3.5 million Sydney residents were forced to boil their water in August and September 1998 after high levels of contamination by giardia and cryptosporidium were discovered in tap-water.

This dramatic cliff collapse is one of three on Burragorang Walls, overlooking the central part of Lake Burragorang. It was caused not by natural processes but by undermining as a result of coal extraction. Coalmining in the area declined after the early 1980s in the face of competition from open-cut mines in the Hunter Valley.

The faeces of all animals, including humans, carry both parasites. Although dead dogs and even ducks were blamed initially, a later investigation fingered the water-testing process itself.)

Mark fired up the engines, turned the twin-hulled Sydney Water craft towards the west and accelerated away. The skeletons of dead trees pointed into the sky from the shallows. Presently we passed the headland where we'd stopped our vehicle at the end of Scotts Main Range road. Opposite stood Pearces Mountain, a 2.5 km long mesa with a generous skirt of bush. Before the lake existed, the road to Wentworth Falls used to climb from the valley to the summit of the mountain via the Jumpback Pass, or the One in Four. At the summit, from McMahons Lookout, travellers could enjoy a magnificent view of the valley they'd just left. These days, the lookout is one of only two offering a sight of the lake to motorists.

We returned to Junction Point and sped down the lake's southern arm. The bluffs of the Burragorang Tableland and Snake Mountains floated smoothly past like gigantic battleships. Those high walls, the cause of the Burragorang's isolation, had collapsed in three places as a result of coalmining underneath them. Mining declined in the early 1980s in the face of competition from open-cut mines in the Hunter Valley.

At Tonalli Cove we pulled into the shore near a waiting 4WD vehicle. Jumping ashore I shook hands with Tony Kondek, also a Sydney Water production officer. As the boat sped away to the north, Tony, a pony-tailed Koori (as south-eastern and Tasmanian Aboriginals call themselves), drove us round the southern end of the lake, past the remains of homesteads and the pile of rubble that was once the Upper Burragorang Co-operative Cheese Factory. What stands out most in my mind about the drive is the huge mobs of eastern grey kangaroos we saw in the former paddocks. They bounced away in all directions at our approach.

After a couple of hours we reached Burragorang Lookout, on the Snake Mountains, the second spot from which motorists are legally able to see the lake. Many say the lake is not half as wonderful as the valley it drowned. But in the same breath they concede that the lake's creation has saved a lot of wild country.

It was dusk when our party of four adults and two youngsters reached the Kowmung River. We'd set off in the mid-morning from Kanangra Walls for a four-day bushwalk led by Patrick Thompson, 51, a Kanangra country veteran. The others in the party were Caroline Begg, Janet Mayer – both fit and experienced walkers – Patrick's 12-year-old daughter, Sarah Ellyard, and my son, Nicholas, 11.

For most of the day squalls had been drifting over from the south, but by the time we'd dropped from the Gingra Range the sky had cleared to a rich midwinter blue. The 400 m deep valley lay in dense shadow when we finally stepped down to a welcome grassy flat on the riverbank, our calf muscles on fire after the ever-steepening descent. A small forest of river oaks thickened the shadow. Here the river was wide and slow, having been fed by good rain. This was a mature river, a far cry from the creek that Don and I had forded earlier.

I was now immersed in the wild country I'd been glimpsing during the past weeks. At this point the Kowmung marks the boundary between Kanangra-Boyd NP to the west and the Blue Mountains NP to the east. The Kanangra-Boyd Wilderness straddles both parks, taking up nearly all of the western park's 68,000 ha and 52,000 ha, or 21 per cent, of the eastern park.

I could well understand Barrallier's grim mood on 26 November 1802 when he reached the Kowmung, this unexpected ravine between Scotts Main Range and Kanangra Tops. By now his party of two Aboriginals and five Europeans was dispirited and running short of supplies. Nevertheless, they reportedly pushed on up Christys Creek, a tributary of the Kowmung, and then up Wheengee Whungee Creek. Beyond a series of waterfalls on 27 November 1802, they halted beneath Johnston Falls. Their morale low, their boots torn and their feet bleeding, they concluded there was no way round the obstacle, so they turned back. Barrallier's diary of his journey, written in French, was confusing and Governor King commissioned George Caley to verify the route in 1804. Meticulous though Caley was, he did not leave a record indicating that he reached Johnston Falls.

As we sat around the campfire, Patrick told Sarah and Nick that, once they had walked along the Kowmung and climbed out, they would be members of a small, élite group and could boast about the feat for the rest of their lives. I was hoping to be able to do that myself.

Dawn showed me the Kowmung as a mass of river oak reflections on chocolate-coloured water. Everywhere I looked I saw only river, trees and sky. It was astonishingly wild and yet, as we trekked downstream that morning, negotiating rocky banks between bright-green flats, I began to get hints that I was just one of a long line of visitors to this place, human and otherwise.

On the flats we came across cattle and horse dung and saw the excavations made by pigs. This did not surprise me: I knew that cattle had been grazed on the river from

Picnic at Storm Stallion Point. Bushwalkers (clockwise from left) Janet Mayer, Patrick Thompson, Caroline Begg, Sarah Ellyard, 12, and Nicholas Meredith, 11, grab a welcome bite during their trek from Kanangra Walls to the Kowmung River. The rocky outcrop, on the edge of Kanangra Tops, overlooks the Arabanoo Creek valley. From here the track winds around to the east and gives access to several parts of the Kowmung, a jewel of a river flowing through some of the wildest country to be found anywhere in Australia.

PETER MEREDITH

PETER MEREDITH

River oaks (above) shade grassy banks on a quiet reach of the Kowmung River, favourite destination of self-sufficient bushwalkers since Myles Dunphy fell in love with it in 1912. The Kowmung became the centre of Myles' conservation focus, epitomising for him not only the beauty of Australia's wilderness but also its fragility in the face of exploitation by timber-getters, cattle-graziers, hunters and miners. Nicholas Meredith (above right) fords Gingra Creek, a tributary of the Kowmung, ahead of Caroline Begg and Sarah Ellyard.

at least the 1860s and that part of it had later been used as a route for stock travelling from Oberon, via Kanangra Tops and the Gingra Range, to the Coxs River. Cattlemen cleared trees from the riverbanks to encourage grass to grow. Some of the cattle and horses, needless to say, stayed behind after the national parks were created.

I asked Patrick if he thought a landscape that had had this much use could legitimately be called a wilderness.

"I don't think there's anywhere left on the planet that can truly be considered pristine wilderness," he replied. "The key point is whether it's capable of restoration, whether it can recover. Although cattlemen, gold fossickers and cedar-getters have left their mark here, the land is recovering."

And he made the point I'd already heard more than once: that here, only 100 km from Sydney, a city of 4 million people, you could be surrounded by wild lands where you would meet few souls other than a handful of adventurers. "It is spectacular country, a bushwalker's paradise," he said.

After struggling to keep up on the first day, the youngsters were romping ahead of the adults by the end of the second. Without much sun in the steep-sided valley, the dewy vegetation hardly dried out at all by day. By evening we were soaked from the waist down. We camped on a grassy river flat, a soft breeze singing in the river oaks, rapids echoing in the steep-sided valley.

Next morning we crawled into our sodden clothes and continued to the junction of the Kowmung and Gingra Creek. By now we'd crossed to the eastern bank of the river. Looking across to the other side, we spotted two parties of bushwalkers on a semi-cleared flat where cedar-getters once camped. The first cedar was probably logged on the Kowmung at about the same time as the cattlemen began using the river. At first the timber was floated downstream (when there was enough water) as far as Penrith, but after the Cedar Road was built in 1907, it was hauled out with horse teams. From the causeway where the road crossed the Kowmung, a network of logging tracks spread up into the valleys to the west.

A fast-flowing section of the Kowmung River near its junction with Gingra Creek. Together with the Wollondilly and the Coxs rivers, the Kowmung is a major source of water for Lake Burragorang. Officially, the first white man to see the river was explorer Francis Barrallier, who crossed it in 1802 in a failed attempt to find a way through the Blue Mountains. He was followed by George Caley in 1806.

NO PINES ON THE BOYD

Even before the 1968–74 campaign to prevent mining in the Colong Caves area was over, the Colong Committee turned its attention to a Forestry Commission plan to log the remaining native trees in Konangaroo State Forest, in the centre of the Boyd Plateau, and to establish a 5000 ha pine plantation there.

The State forest lay south-east of Jenolan Caves and straddled the Jenolan–Kanangra road outside the Kanangra-Boyd NP, which had been declared in 1969. Conservationists were demanding that it be included in the park, as Myles Dunphy had intended.

As happened during the Colong campaign, public opinion forced the Government's hand. In 1974 it set up an inquiry by the State Pollution Control Commission, which recommended against pine planting and "further damage to the natural environment within the Konangaroo State Forest". The State forest was added to the park in 1977.

A patch of the eucalypt woodland that once blanketed the landscape survives in a sea of plantation pine in Vulcan State Forest, near Shooters Hill, outside the western perimeter of Kanangra-Boyd National Park.

Today you'll find a concrete weir (with an awkward gap in the centre) across the Kowmung where the Cedar Road used to cross, as well as a Sydney Water hut and gauging station that records river flow and height. By the time we reached the weir, the other walkers had gathered opposite to watch us cross. I took my boots off to ford the wide rapids below the weir. When I climbed up the far bank, the spectators – mostly grey-hairs from Bathurst – suggested I not worry about getting my boots wet, since we faced some 50 crossings on Gingra Creek.

They were right. The youngsters kept count, and in the end tallied 54. But the creek scenes – of waterfalls and cascades, pools and rapids, framed by myriad shades of green – that opened up around every bend kept our minds off the cold and damp. Where possible we followed the remains of a cedar-getters' track, called Gingra Creek Road. In places it was beautifully built, forming wide, solid ledges on steep gully sides; in other places it vanished altogether.

We climbed onto the Gingra Range on the fourth day and arrived back at Kanangra Tops after sunset. Fit and seemingly full of energy after their 45 km walk, the youngsters continually had to be told to wait for the toiling adults. Finally, just when we felt we'd never cover the last few hundred metres, we were inspired by a glorious sight. A rising full moon had dusted the walls of the gorge with silver. We stopped to stare. I thought: no wonder Myles Dunphy felt strongly enough about the place to name his first son Milo Kanangra.

AFTER MY KANANGRA WALK, I wanted to find out what was being done about feral animals in national parks. I discovered that though they are being given a hard time, in the end they may never be eradicated entirely.

In a clearing on the Boyd Plateau, high in the Kowmung's catchment, I contemplated a pig that lay dead near the trap in which it had been caught. With its coat of black hair and heavy tusks, it did not bear much resemblance to a farm porker.

It was a cold, wet morning. I'd been brought to this muddy spot off the Jenolan–Kanangra road by Mick English, NPWS senior field supervisor based at Oberon, and his assistant, Mark McLean. Mick, whose well-trimmed beard-and-moustache combination gave him the air of a Victorian gentleman, was busy testing the trap, a 2 m square pen with a vertical door released by a trip-wire.

Parks staff know of at least 13 exotic animal species inside the Blue Mountains parks, including cattle, horses, goats, dogs, pigs, foxes, cats and rabbits. The biggest menace are the pigs, and their impact has been growing steadily for more than a decade.

Mick told me that although when he started working for the NPWS 10 years ago he was mainly using traps in the campaign against pigs, nowadays poisoning with 1080 was proving more efficient. "We bait and then use trapping as a follow-up," he said.

All around the trap I could see the pigs' handiwork. The clearing looked as though it had been torn up by earthmoving machinery. The furrows were full of muddy rainwater, and the implications of this were plain to see at another site that Mick took me to.

NPWS senior field supervisor Mick English (left) checks damage caused by feral pigs to a creek flat on the Boyd Plateau. Rainwater will carry the resulting silt from here into the Kowmung River and eventually to Lake Burragorang. Some of the pigs in Kanangra-Boyd National Park are probably descended from animals that escaped from surrounding farms; others may have been introduced to the area by hunters. Mick examines a feral pig (below) shot during an eradication campaign.

We picked up supplies of grain from a store of drums off the Oberon–Kanangra road and then walked through a dripping woodland of snow gum and peppermint to a lush meadow. Here the damage stood out against the vivid green. And right through the middle ran a creek, cloudy with mud. In a week or two, the water would reach Lake Burragorang.

Mick said he and colleagues had poisoned an estimated 150 pigs on the Boyd Plateau in 1997. "I always thought that if we could knock out the population around here they wouldn't spread to other areas," he said. "But I got it wrong. They're on the Kowmung, Scotts Main Range, under Wentworth Falls and around Yerranderie and Lake Burragorang."

Ian Brown, NPWS district operations manager based at the service's Blue Mountains headquarters in Blackheath, told me later that the pig population had grown noticeably in the southern Blue Mountains in the past five years, probably radiating from the Boyd. Since I knew that the NPWS aimed to eradicate feral animals from parks where possible ("with emphasis on those with a high invasive potential", according to a draft management plan), I asked him how feasible this policy was.

"The best we could hope for is to get rid of those creatures that can be got rid of and to keep the rest down to a low-impact level, because with methods other than biological control it's the last couple of animals that cost the most," Ian said.

The vast chamber of the Devil's Coachhouse, at Jenolan Caves, dwarfs a solitary visitor. This cavern greets backpackers coming from Katoomba on the Six Foot Track. In the mid-1800s tourists arriving on horseback would camp here and in the nearby Grand Arch. They were advised to wear old clothes when exploring the caves, and part of the fun of a Jenolan visit was being able to dress in clothes that masked one's social status. One woman recalled the pleasure of wearing "a dreadful skirt that made me look like some disreputable charwoman".

ADVENTURE UNDERGROUND

In the 1800s, visitors to Jenolan Caves, then one of inland Australia's most popular tourist attractions, expected the journey there to be as exciting as the destination.

From the late 1840s, parties rode from Bathurst, Oberon or Tarana, many having travelled from Sydney via Hartley. They might overnight on the Whalan property, 20 km from the caves. Pastoralist James Whalan had discovered the caves in 1838 and had explored them regularly since. He led the groups from his homestead for the day's ride through dramatic scenery to Jenolan.

The visitors camped in the two large open caverns, the Grand Arch and the Devil's Coachhouse. Wearing rough clothes and carrying candles, they crawled and stumbled through the passages until exhausted and bruised. Typically, they spent three days there.

Later, trains carried visitors to Mount Victoria, and subsequently Tarana, where they boarded buggies for the rest of the journey. In 1884, the Six Foot Track linked the caves directly with Katoomba, enabling fast walkers to reach them in a day. As roads improved and car ownership spread, the rail link was used less and less.

A thriving colony of brush-tailed rock wallabies (left) became one of the attractions of a visit to Jenolan after the caves were discovered in 1838. But inappropriate food, deaths in road accidents, hunting for sport, and competition with feral goats soon caused their numbers to plummet. Today a mere 15 survive in an enclosure that protects them from foxes and cats. Visitors to Jenolan Caves c. 1910 (below left) enjoyed the comfort of a motoring trip.

The NSW Government officially reserved Jenolan Caves in 1866. Jeremiah Wilson, their first keeper, built a six-room rest house in 1880 and gradually expanded it until, in 1898, the Government added a limestone wing and named it Caves House. It added another wing in 1914, and by 1923 the guesthouse, accommodating 200, looked much as it does today. In 1990, the Government put the guesthouse out for tender. It is now run by Jenolan Caves Resort Pty Ltd.

The Jenolan system comprises 300 caves. Nine caves have been developed for tourism, and these, with their bright lighting, concrete paths and steel steps, attract more than 270,000 visitors a year. The trouble, as far as the management of Caves House is concerned, is that, unlike the hardy adventurers of the 1800s, most of those visitors come only for the day. The guesthouse and its outbuildings have undergone a major restoration, and management hopes to entice visitors to stay longer by offering a menu of adventurous activities.

At Jenolan Caves, about 15 km to the north, I was given an insight of the havoc that other pest animals can wreak on our wildlife. The area had been home to a healthy colony of brush-tailed rock wallabies when the caves were discovered by Europeans in 1838 and the endearing marsupials had soon become part of the attraction for the growing numbers of tourists. But inappropriate food given by visitors, road deaths and hunting took a heavy toll. The wallabies also had to compete increasingly with goats for food and shelter.

By the early 1960s Jenolan staff were worried at the noticeable decline in wallaby numbers. In 1964 they built a 0.5 ha compound into which they eventually herded one male and three female wallabies for their protection. By 1980 the captive colony had grown to 80–90. In 1988, after an outbreak of the debilitating disease lumpy jaw, the NPWS decided the compound was becoming too crowded (even though it had been expanded to 2.5 ha) and ordered their release.

"So they were released, but unfortunately nobody realised how bad the fox and cat problem was," said John Callaghan, a senior guide at the caves who showed me around the compound – three interlinked enclosures covering 7.5 ha and protected by a 2.4 m high electrified fence – above McKeons Creek. Foxes killed the adults, while cats took joeys just out of the pouch.

By the early 1990s the local wallaby population had plummeted. To prevent their extinction in the area, the survivors were trapped in 1992 and returned to the compound. From the five that survived the initial period in captivity, the colony has grown to 15.

The Jenolan Caves Reserve Trust, the body that administers the caves area, set up a committee in 1992 to oversee the wallabies' care. The colony has been closely monitored, in part through an AUSTRALIAN GEOGRAPHIC-backed study. The brush-tailed rock wallaby, common throughout the State in the 1800s, is now rare and vulnerable. The Jenolan colony, small though it is, is among the last in south-eastern Australia.

Ernst Holland, chairman of the committee, told me the prospects for their eventual release are quite good. "Our extensive cat- and fox-control programs appear very effective," he said.

These days few visitors to Jenolan know of the rock wallabies' sad plight. Caves are what people come to see, and here they can find some of the most spectacular in the world. I've toured a number of them over the past 15 years, and I never fail to come away utterly amazed.

At the Jenolan guides' office during my most recent visit, I happened to overhear that a geologist was working in one of the cave systems. Jumping at the opportunity to find out about the caves from a scientist, I persuaded guide Doug Williamson to take me underground.

As we hurried through River Cave, considered the most strenuous of Jenolan's systems to visit because of its 1298 steps, Doug flicked on lights ahead of us and

Caves House (opposite), looking like a transplanted Swiss ski resort, nestles in a deep blind valley near the Jenolan River gorge. Nine of Jenolan's 300 caves have been developed for tourism, with extensive lighting, concrete paths and steps, steel stairways and handrails. The caves are filled with a staggering array of formations that makes them among the most beautiful in the world. The Persian Chamber (above) in Orient Cave contains the 10 m tall Pillar of Hercules, Jenolan's highest known stalagmite.

The Pool of Cerberus (above), named after the mythical three-headed dog that guarded the entrance to Hades, is part of an underground river. The tour through the cave takes 90 minutes and is strenuous but well worth the effort. University of Sydney geologist Armstrong Osborne (opposite above) measures the angle of a layer of rock as part of a study he hopes will confirm his theory about the formation of Jenolan Caves'. This sooty owl (opposite below), pictured in one of the caves at Jenolan, is one of a line that may have been roosting there for 17,000 years. A pile of bones beneath the roosting site contains relics of small mammals now extinct.

switched them off behind. At last we burst into a domed chamber where, under an arch, three silhouetted figures were stooped in work.

They were Armstrong Osborne, of the School of Professional Studies at the University of Sydney, and Brad Pillans and John Chappell, from the Australian National University in Canberra. We were in the Mud Tunnel at the base of the Olympia Steps. The spotlit Grand Column, one of Jenolan's best-known features, floated above us like a frozen fountain.

Armstrong, a short, stocky figure with a gnomish beard, immediately began to explain his project with a zealot's enthusiasm. For a long time he had been suspicious about the standard explanation of the caves' formation, he said. It had always been thought that the limestone in which the caves formed was deposited in a sea about 400 million years ago, and that geological upheavals eventually lifted the limestone above sea level. Rainwater made slightly acid by the absorption of airborne carbon dioxide then trickled through cracks and faults in the rock, dissolving it and creating caves. Roof collapses and erosion by water-borne solids accelerated the process.

But Armstrong theorises that after the first caves were formed, they were flooded with seawater and filled anew with limestone. The sea level then dropped (or the rock rose) once more and the new limestone became subject to the same processes that had created the original caves. This happened more than once.

"So we've got a history of caves forming and then getting filled up and then new caves forming inside the old ones," Armstrong said.

He pointed to the arch above us. "This rock here is inside an ancient cave. It's limestone too, but it's very much younger than the 400-million-year-old rock – about 320 million years old, we think. So we're looking at the younger infill of a very ancient cave. At Jenolan we've probably got something like five different eras of cave development, all overprinted on one another. Sorting them out is very complicated."

To help them in their task, the scientists were taking samples of rock that they would date using a process that measures the rock's magnetic direction. The Earth's magnetic field makes a permanent imprint on rock, and since the field's alignment has changed quite dramatically over the aeons, determining an imprint's direction can indicate a rock's age. The technique is known as palaeomagnetic dating.

Armstrong's explanation for the caves' formation is not revolutionary. It has been applied to caves elsewhere in the world, but not to Jenolan. "I'm trying to piece together a new history of the caves which recognises where everything fits in," he said. "It's important for the interpretation given to tourists."

Back above ground, I ran into a group of bushwalkers outside Caves House, the elegant Victorian guesthouse that gives the Jenolan Valley such a surprisingly Swiss look. They had just walked the 42 km Six Foot Track from Katoomba. I envied them. I fancied a good walk, especially one on a track with such a long and interesting history. But it was time to use another form of transport with an equally fascinating history in the Blue Mountains.

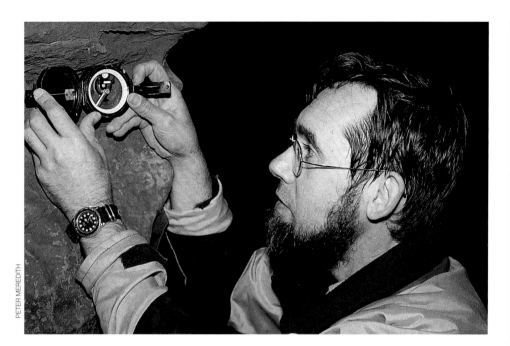

PETER MEREDITH

DAVID HOLLANDS

TRAVEL ADVICE

Scotts Main Range Road is closed to horseriders and unauthorised vehicles but open to bushwalkers and mountain-bikers. For further information, contact the NPWS's Blue Mountains headquarters in Blackheath (see p. 41) or the Confederation of Bushwalking Clubs of NSW, ☎ 02 9548 1228, <www.bushwalking.org.au>.

The prohibited zone around Lake Burragorang is entirely out of bounds except for the two lookouts that motorists can reach (see p. 48) and two bushwalking corridors, one at the southern end of the lake and the other between Scotts Main Range and Wild Dog Mountains. Contact Sydney Water, ☎ 02 4720 0349, for information on recreational facilities at Warragamba Dam.

Jenolan Caves can be reached by road from the Great Western Highway, turn off at Hartley. For information on Jenolan Caves tours, contact the guides' office, ☎ 02 6359 3311. Caves House offers a range of accommodation, from classic to budget, ☎ 02 6359 3322, numerous websites.

A marker sign on the Six Foot Track, whose name derives from its original width. The track crosses private farmland in places and walkers should avoid disturbing stock, damaging property or straying from the path. Allow 2–3 days for the walk.

Edge of eternity

The lower mountains

"There's no better way to travel, thundering along with this great fire in it – it's almost like it's alive." They were the words of a committed steam buff. We were on a steam train and you could pick out the buffs: serious men holding microphones or tape recorders out of windows to capture the sounds of a lost age. But this was no ordinary steam buff.

Petite and vivacious, Jenni Edmonds, 24, wore her waist-length hair knotted under her engine driver's cap. Jenni has been a self-confessed steam addict since childhood, when her father would pick family holiday destinations near steam railways. At the time I met her she was studying mechanical engineering at the Sydney Institute of Technology while working at Sydney's Powerhouse Museum as an apprentice fitter and machinist.

From 1994 Jenni helped with the museum's restoration of 3830 ("thirty-eight-thirty"), the last of the great 38-class steam locomotives that served NSW from 1943 to the late 1960s. The restoration was a joint venture between the museum and 3801 Limited, a non-profit company that runs locomotive 3801 ("thiry-eight-o-one") and a fleet of historic carriages. Locomotive 3830, recommissioned in 1997 after a five-year refit, serves as a back-up for the 3801 and was the loco hauling us to the

Blue Mountains on one of the company's regular steam tours.

Jenni was enjoying every minute of the journey on "her" train. And she was absolutely right: there *is* no better way to travel. I'd had an inkling of this back at Sydney's Central Station. The moment the packed train began to pull out, hampers were opened, scones were slathered with cream, and champagne corks popped. Everyone was out to have a good time.

Through Sydney's western suburbs we thundered, tongues of steam and smoke licking at the rattling windows and filling carriages with the aromas of boiling water, burning coal and hot paintwork. The loco's chuffing and mournful whistle echoed off passing buildings. Beyond Penrith the landscape became greener and the Blue Mountains bluer.

Arthur Phillip, governor of the fledgling NSW colony, was the first settler to sight the mountains. While exploring north of Port Jackson in 1788, he caught sight of them from the site of present-day Pennant Hills. Those in the north he named the Carmarthen Hills and those in the south the Lansdowne Hills. Others ignored these names and referred to the mountains by the name used today.

Drought and a shortage of land compelled gentleman farmer Gregory Blaxland (centre) to look beyond the Blue Mountains for more room for his cattle enterprise. With two other landholders – William Wentworth (right) and William Lawson (far right) – four servants, five dogs and five horses, he set out on 11 May 1813 to find a route across. It took the expeditioners just two weeks to achieve what so many before them had failed to do.

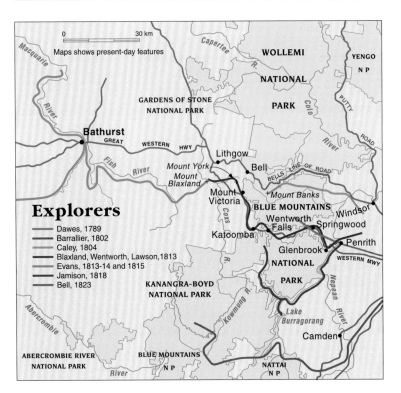

Explorers

—— Dawes, 1789
—— Barrallier, 1802
—— Caley, 1804
—— Blaxland, Wentworth, Lawson, 1813
—— Evans, 1813-14 and 1815
—— Jamison, 1818
—— Bell, 1823

For more than 20 years the mountains presented what seemed an insuperable barrier to the colony's expansion westward, though Aboriginals had crossed them regularly for millennia. After a succession of failed forays, mainly into the gorges, a drought forced the colonists to set out in search of new pastures for their livestock. Gregory Blaxland, Lieutenant William Lawson of the NSW Corps and William Wentworth mounted an expedition in 1813. Sticking to the ridges, they reached 1061 m high Mount York, near the present-day village of Mount Victoria, in 15 days. Three days later they were standing on Mount Blaxland, 10 km further west. The route they had taken followed very closely that of the Great Western Highway today.

Sceptical, Governor Lachlan Macquarie sent surveyor George Evans to confirm the expedition's achievement. Evans reached Mount Blaxland in eight days and pushed on a further 50 km to the plains around present-day Bathurst.

The newly discovered grazing lands could not be exploited without a road. William Cox, chief magistrate at Windsor, built one in six months during 1814–15, using convict labour to grub, hoe, dig and blast a way through the scrub. Over subsequent decades, the road was improved and realigned in a number of places. Even so, travel remained difficult and dangerous (initially because of attacks by Aboriginals) until the railway arrived. Only the most determined traveller was prepared to make the three-week trek to Bathurst, though traffic became heavy after 1851, when gold was discovered near there. Other than a string of inns, military depots and coaching facilities, there was little development along the road. In 1823, Archibald Bell, aged 19, discovered a second route through the mountains, allegedly with the help of an

Aboriginal woman. Today Bells Line of Road offers motorists a less-urbanised alternative to the Great Western Highway.

West of the Nepean River, the 3830 began to climb. Leaving neat housing estates on the lower slopes, it was soon weaving through bush. Gaps in the vegetation offered views across a sea of treed suburbs to a grey blanket of smog in the east. Then, in a startling transition, we emerged from a cutting into a classic Blue Mountains gully, all tumbled sandstone cliffs embedded in dense vegetation. We were on the northern side of Glenbrook Gorge. The change took my breath away. But more was to come.

The train thundered into a tunnel. As it exploded from the other end, the foreground detail fell away to leave an uncluttered panorama of blue-green bush under a cool sky. I was looking towards the Blue Labyrinth, in the central part of Blue Mountains NP.

Glenbrook is the second village you reach as you travel up the mountains on the Great Western Highway or by train. Like many in the mountains, its station has an old-world charm brightened by well-tended flowerbeds. And, as with other towns in the lower Blue Mountains, a large percentage of its 5600 or so residents commute to Sydney. That's not to deny its charm. I lived here for two years in the 1980s. I swam in Jellybean Pool, just inside the national park; I camped at Euroka Clearing,

Lines of communication (above left). The 3830 draws into Penrith station on its way up to the Blue Mountains during one of the regular steam tours run by 3801 Ltd, a non-profit company that operates historic trains. Last of the 38-class steam locomotives that were phased out in the late 1960s, the 3830 was recommissioned in 1997 after a five-year refit by Sydney's Powerhouse Museum. The railway line through the mountains, built between 1863 and 1869, opened up the region to development and tourism and paved the way for the predominantly car-based tourist industry that exists today. Engineering student and apprentice fitter Jenni Edmonds (above right) watches in the cab as fireman Warren Lloyd takes the 3830 through the Glenbrook tunnel.

The oldest bridge on mainland Australia, Lennox Bridge (above) spans Lapstone Creek above Emu Plains, on the Blue Mountains' eastern escarpment. Completed in 1833, it carried all the traffic to NSW's west until 1926. Its builder, David Lennox, was a master mason. Blue Mountains historian Jim Barrett (above right) and wife Pat take a break while exploring the abandoned railway cutting above the Lapstone zigzag. The disused Glenbrook railway tunnel (opposite), in operation from 1892 till 1913, is today the site of the mushroom-growing enterprise of Mushroom Biotech, run by Dechang Sun. The company produces shimeji and shiitaki mushrooms for local and overseas consumption.

explored Glenbrook Gorge and did the two-and-a-half-hour return walk to Red Hands Cave. But, as I was about to find out, I missed a lot.

Historian Jim Barrett, author of a handful of books on the southern Blue Mountains, reckons Glenbrook is the most interesting of the mountains' settlements apart from Katoomba. He should know: he began bushwalking in the area as a member of the Catholic Bushwalking Club in 1948 and he and his wife Pat have lived here for 38 years. When I met him he had a leg in a brace as a result of a bushwalking knee injury. He is a laconic man, with a reticent though heartfelt smile. He and Pat took me to places around Glenbrook that I never knew existed. The first was the zigzag near the neighbouring village of Lapstone.

In 1861 John Whitton, engineer-in-chief of the NSW Railways, proposed extending the western line beyond Penrith through the mountains to Bathurst. Taking the line up the escarpment from Emu Plains was the first of several major engineering obstacles he faced. Tunnels would have mitigated the incline but were too expensive. The only solution was a zigzag.

Work began on the Lapstone zigzag and a viaduct over Knapsack Gully in 1863. Soon it was being hailed as one of Australia's greatest engineering feats, though eventually it would be eclipsed by Whitton's masterpiece, the Great Zig Zag on the other side of the mountains.

Jim and Pat led me along a neat cutting, now mostly overgrown, on the zigzag's top level. Jim explained how the zigzag worked. It had three inclined levels linked by two sets of points. A train coming from Emu Plains would go up the first level, past the first set of points and along a siding to a dead end. The points would switch the train onto the second level. It would then reverse up this 1-in-33 incline to a second siding and dead end, where the second set of points would direct it forwards onto the top level. From there the line swept around to the west along the present route of the Great Western Highway, Glenbrook station then being where the village's petrol station now stands beside the highway.

We walked to "Top Points" on the edge of Knapsack Gully for a view of the viaduct. "This zigzag achieved world renown," Jim said. "And Whitton's viaduct is probably the most beautiful ever built in Australia. Further up, near a cottage once used by artist Arthur Streeton, the train would crawl so slowly up the gradient that, in Streeton's day, children could run alongside and hand apples up to the fireman and the driver on sticks and in return they could get a lift to school in Glenbrook."

Just off the highway, about a kilometre east of the Glenbrook service station, Pat showed me the weed-clogged entrance of a disused tunnel. The tunnel was built in 1892 as part of a deviation to ease congestion on the zigzag and reduce the gradient.

"The tunnel leaked, it was dark and narrow and had poor ventilation, and both crew and passengers were almost asphyxiated when the train went through. It was a real horror trip," Jim told me back at the car.

The tunnel became redundant in 1913 when the present line through Glenbrook Gorge was opened, reducing the gradient from 1-in-33 to 1-in-60.

MOUNTAIN BLUES

The haze over the Blue Mountains is said to be of a deeper blue than any other in the world. According to John Low, Blue Mountains City Library's local studies librarian, the Blue Mountains City Council became so frustrated at being unable to answer the frequent questions about the colour that in 1955 it consulted physicist Harry Messel, then at the University of Sydney.

Harry replied that the haze that appears to surround a distant object is due to "Rayleigh scattering", the scattering or reflection of sunlight by floating particles such as dust, water droplets and even air molecules. The sun illuminates these particles, and the eye sees them collectively as haze.

Harry postulated that, since tiny droplets of oil scatter sunlight more effectively than most particles, the deeper blue is due to the fine mist of oil droplets dispersed into the air by the millions of gum trees in the mountains.

MAKING PASSES

The word "pass", when used in a geographical context, usually means a negotiable gap through a mountain barrier, as in the Khyber Pass. That's not generally how it's used in the Blue Mountains.

Many of the round-trip tracks in the central Blue Mountains started out as two or more separate one-way walks to the bases of waterfalls. Realising that a round trip was more attractive to visitors, the trustees of the early reserves would often link waterfall tracks by means of a track that came to be known as a "pass". The first was probably Rodriguez Pass, at Blackheath, named in 1900 after Thomas Rodriguez, a local businessman. Among the more outstanding of the Blue Mountains passes are the National Pass at Wentworth Falls and the Federal Pass at Katoomba.

Not all of the Blue Mountains passes conform to this definition. Victoria Pass, for instance, is the steep descent from Mount Victoria on the western side of the Blue Mountains escarpment. And Pierces Pass is a ravine that provides access into the Grose Gorge from the Bell Range.

German visitors Kerstin and Mathias Steinberg walk the Federal Pass, built in 1900 with money donated by Katoomba businesses to attract tourists. It covers some 4 km between Leura Forest and Katoomba Falls.

CONVENIENCE COMPELLED ME to use electric trains for most of my travels on the Blue Mountains line. I missed the noise, smoke and steam – even the soot in my eyes – but I appreciated the comfort of the modern service.

Above Glenbrook it struck me how insignificant humanity's artefacts – its buildings, roads and railway lines – appeared beside the solidity of the surrounding landscape. Wherever I looked from the train I saw views of seemingly endless rolling forest. And in the foreground, hemmed in by trees, stood clusters of buildings that I felt the landscape could shrug off at any moment. One had only to walk a few hundred metres in any direction to reach the edge of "civilisation" and be able to stare into a past that goes back aeons – so far that, for all intents and purposes, it is eternity.

At the village of Warrimoo, two stops from Glenbrook, I did more than just stare. From the station I walked down tree-lined Florabella Street to where it ended abruptly at scrub. On a narrow footpath, I stepped through the greenery and immediately found myself at the edge. The path fell steeply, giving me a view through the trees into a gorge. The further down I walked, the moister the forest became until, on the creek, I was walking though rainforest among ferns and moss-covered boulders. The howl of traffic on the highway had faded to nothing. I felt I'd stumbled, like Alice, through a looking-glass into a parallel world. For an hour or two, I could be alone in eternity.

The two-hour Florabella Pass walk from Warrimoo to Blaxland was a treat. It is one of the many privately built tracks that drop from the edge along the urban strip. It was the brainchild of Sir Arthur Rickard, a developer active in the Warrimoo area in 1918–25. When writing *Blinky Bill Grows Up* in 1940, children's author Dorothy Wall was inspired by the bush she saw on the track.

Beyond the moist gorge the track met Glenbrook Creek, where sandstone crags glowed in the afternoon sun. Sooner than I wanted, I was back on the highway at Blaxland, exhilarated to realise that scores of similar walks – some shorter, some more adventurous – waited for me up the line.

As the train took me into Springwood, I sighted the edge again. Springwood grew from a military barracks established in 1816 to a major dormitory town with a population of 7000, the largest settlement in the lower Blue Mountains. But despite the town's size, you can see the edge all around. I had sudden glimpses of it between buildings as I strolled along Macquarie Road, the brash main street.

The panoramic view (opposite) from above Wentworth Falls that so impressed Charles Darwin remains as outstanding today as when he saw it in 1836. With the western cliffs of Kings Tableland enclosing what resembles a bay, it is not surprising Darwin theorised that aeons ago the sea filled the valley. Despite this error, water does dominate in this environment, as part of the "bay's" name – Valley of the Waters – implies.

HAROLD CAZNEAUX/MITCHELL LIBRARY, STATE LIBRARY OF NEW SOUTH WALES

The naked forms of strong, well-built women dominate in Norman Lindsay's artistic works. The garden of his 16 ha estate (above), now the site of the Norman Lindsay Gallery, at Faulconbridge, is dotted with figures he created after he bought the property in 1912. Lindsay and Rose Soady (above right) developed a highly productive creative partnership. Not only was she his chief model and later his wife, but she also performed tasks he preferred to avoid, like printing his etchings and managing his career.

At Faulconbridge, the next stop up the line, I encountered the edge once more in a most surprising circumstance.

A 45-minute walk from the station brought me to the Norman Lindsay Gallery, the former home of artist Norman Lindsay, now in the hands of the National Trust. Born in 1879, Lindsay was a compulsive illustrator from early childhood. Having made his name as a cartoonist, he took up etching in 1917, creating a body of work considered his finest. In 1918 he published *The Magic Pudding*, still one of Australia's most popular children's books, and later wrote several controversial novels. Although he came to oil painting relatively late in his career, it is for his paintings – and the powerful naked women they depict – that he is renowned.

Lindsay and his favourite model, Rose Soady, bought a small stone cottage in what is now Faulconbridge in 1912 and renovated it themselves. Lindsay did most of the heavy work, delighting in learning new skills and in populating his garden with statues of buxom women. His house, one of the most visited buildings in the Blue Mountains, sits on 16 ha of partly cleared land. Its gardens are spacious, with broad expanses of lawn on which fountains topped with muscular bodies draw the eye. Touring the airy buildings and gardens with Jane Lennon, the gallery's assistant manager, I asked whether the public was more enlightened today about Lindsay's work than in the past. Her answer surprised me.

Although Lindsay built a separate studio (left) on his property, he tended to work in all parts of the main house. He also built an etching studio, which functioned as a privately run café and craft shop next door to the gallery until August 1999, when the National Trust took it over. Lindsay believed his home stood over a chasm leading into hell. This, he claimed, accounted for his compulsive and restless creativity. The bronze statue (below) of a Balinese dancer in a courtyard at the museum is a copy of a concrete original kept in the main house. Art critic Robert Hughes maintained that Lindsay saw Australia as a pagan Arcadia, peopled with characters from mythology and history – goddesses, heroes, fawns, nymphs and satyrs. Though his work exhibits an earthy delight in the human body and life's pleasures, Hughes believes Lindsay was neither evil nor pornographic, just innocently vulgar. He was "as wholesome as a kid", Hughes said. "His nudes are fearsomely maternal."

"Some people are horrified and refuse even to enter the gallery," she said. "Recently the Friends of the Gallery had a stall outside a church during a street parade. They were raffling one of Lindsay's pictures, a nude, and church people complained. It's extraordinary that people still think like that!"

Lindsay worked with prodigious energy almost till the day he died at 90. As well as posing for many of his works, Rose, who married Norman in 1920, managed his finances and printed his etchings. Before his death in 1969, Lindsay left much of his art to the National Trust on condition the trust bought his house and displayed his work in it. He jokingly said this was to ensure he would be remembered as an artist rather than just as the author of *The Magic Pudding*.

I decided to explore the uncleared part of the Lindsay estate. I strolled past a small dam, originally built as a swimming pool, and in a moment was standing on the rim of a gorge, dark and mysterious. I thought: This is typical of these mountains. You step so unexpectedly from suburbia to the very edge of wildness.

IF LINDSAY'S FORMER HOME is a popular icon of the mountains, in the village of Woodford I found another building that deserved to be.

At Woodford station I began to get a sense, for the first time since starting my ascent, of being in mountains rather than on a sloping plain. The view to the north-

The stone-flagged courtyard (top picture) of the Woodford Academy has a barrel-vaulted underground water tank that provided water for patrons when the complex functioned as an inn. The kitchen (above) has a fireplace and a bread oven that are among the finest surviving in NSW. Norah Holman (above right), of the National Trust's Blue Mountains Committee, in one of the inn's public rooms.

west, across to the basalt-capped prominences of Mount Banks, Mount Tomah and Mount Wilson 20–30 km away, was needle-sharp. Immediately below me, the highway's blue-grey expanse swept up to the left, carrying some of the 20,000-plus vehicles that travel on it daily.

Up the hill stands the Woodford Academy, a group of National Trust buildings that are the oldest still standing in the Blue Mountains and one of the most substantial colonial-Victorian inn complexes in NSW. Sly-grogger and ex-convict William James, the first known resident in Twenty Mile Hollow (as Woodford was once called), built a squat here in about 1820. Thomas Pembroke, another ex-convict, was granted legal tenure over James's squat in 1831 to build an inn and erected most of the fine sandstone buildings that stand today. Not long afterwards, James's wife died in sinister circumstances. James was convicted of murder and sentenced to death but had his conviction quashed on appeal.

The buildings served as a guesthouse, inn and private home until 1907, when John Fraser McManamey turned them into the Woodford Academy for Boys. The school closed in 1936 and McManamey's family donated the buildings to the National Trust in 1979.

When I visited, Woodford Academy was very much in need of tender loving care. Tree roots were lifting the front pavers, the roof was disintegrating, damp was threatening artefacts inside, including some paintings, and parts of the complex were unsafe. So I wasn't surprised when Norah Holman, of the National Trust's Blue Mountains Committee, told me income from the monthly open days and occasional guided tours was barely covering costs. However, a recent grant of $1 million from the Federal Government would enable the trust to begin restoration work.

The interior was dim and cold. According to Norah, many people who visit believe it's more than just the cold that gives you goose pimples. She told me about a mentally disabled girl who used to be locked in her room upstairs when visitors came. As the visitors passed by outside, she would tap on the window to attract attention. To this day people occasionally hear tapping at the upstairs window. Others report hearing unintelligible conversations in rooms known to be empty.

"It's a dark, brooding place and on some days you know there is a presence here," Norah said. With her aquiline brows and piercing eyes, she does not seem out of place there herself.

With the frailty of most human artefacts uppermost in my mind, I went four stops up the line to Wentworth Falls. When Cox built his road in 1814–15, he erected a small weatherboard storage hut here beside Jamison Creek. Although the hut burnt down a few years later, the name "Weatherboard" for the settlement stuck till after the railway line arrived in 1867. In the late 1820s, the Weatherboard Inn was built near the creek. One of its early guests was naturalist Charles Darwin, who came here in 1836 during his circumnavigation in HMS *Beagle*. He explored Jamison Creek to where it pours over the cliffs on the edge of the Valley of the Waters in a series of cascades known as Wentworth Falls.

I set off to see what Darwin saw, though I chose Falls Road for my approach. On the way I called in at the Falls Gallery.

Housed in a restored turn-of-the-century weatherboard cottage, the gallery is the home and workplace of printmaker Anne Smith and her husband, Ian, a potter. As well as exhibiting their own work, the couple show the output of other prominent Australian artists including Arthur Boyd, Clifton Pugh, Wendy Sharpe, Garry Shead and Max Miller. Amid a plethora of galleries in the Blue Mountains, the Falls Gallery stands out not only because it specialises in etchings but also because it deals with the work of artists from beyond the mountains.

Artists in residence. Potter Ian Smith (above right), formerly an engineer, and printmaker Anne Smith, who used to work as an electron microscopist, bought a run-down weatherboard cottage in Wentworth Falls village in the late 1980s and have turned it into not just a comfortable home but also a successful gallery. They exhibit their own work as well as that of major Australian artists.

Like the balcony of a giant natural theatre (opposite), the head of Prince Regents Glen is testimony to the erosive power of water. Here Jamison Creek plunges off the escarpment to form Wentworth Falls, probably the most spectacular and beautiful of the many falls in the Blue Mountains. Over aeons the creek – in the foreground at right – has carved its way down through the rock, gradually lengthening the valley. The National Pass can be seen halfway up the cliff at top left. Against the backdrop of the valley's darkening gum forest (left), walkers negotiate the stairs from the top of Wentworth Falls to the middle level. From there they can either return by the same route to the picnic area at the summit or continue along the National Pass. Bernhard Paul and Martina Huber (above) make their way towards the top of the stairs.

Artists and travellers have been portraying the Blue Mountains from the earliest days of settlement. Some have passed through; others (like the Smiths and Reinis Zusters, who lives nearby) have settled.

Zusters' studio overlooks Jamison Creek. His painting "Darwin's Walk" depicts visitors retracing the great naturalist's route. When Darwin reached the falls he was astounded at the sight that met his eyes: " ... suddenly & without any preparation, through the trees, which border the pathway, an immense gulf is seen at the depth of perhaps 1500 ft [450 m] beneath one's feet. Walking a few yards further, one stands on the brink of a precipice. Below is the grand bay or gulf, for I know not what other name to give it, thickly covered with forest."

I wanted to approach the falls from the western arm of the Valley of the Waters, along the National Pass. This track was one of a number in the Jamison Valley that were developed between the 1860s and the 1930s by what Blue Mountains walking-track historian Jim Smith has called "a creative partnership between the State Government and local community organisations".

At the end of Fletcher Street I visited the NPWS Conservation Hut, an airy, rammed-earth café that in 1991 replaced a tea-room built in 1905. Here, beneath two wall-sized Zusters paintings, I had my eyes opened.

Kanangra Walls may have been inspiring, but the vista of the Valley of the Waters and the Jamison Valley that fell away beneath the café's windows filled me with profoundest awe. Darwin aptly described the valley as being like a vast cliff-ringed bay, with bush where the sea should have been and the cliffs marching from one headland to another into the distance. The effect, for me, was of arriving in a spacecraft over an alien but beautiful planet after a long spell of humdrum intergalactic flight.

The National Pass, one of the most spectacular walks in the Blue Mountains, is a tribute to the ingenuity and bravery of the early track makers. A steep descent took me from eucalypt woodland around the Conservation Hut into temperate rainforest around Valley of Waters Creek. From there I stepped onto a ledge – formed by a shallow horizontal layer of red claystone sandwiched between two vast masses of

Having cooled off in the pool (left) at the base of Wentworth Falls, these two visitors will warm up again on the hard climb to the top. Over 2 million people visit the Katoomba region every year and take advantage of a track and lookout system dating from the 1800s. As early as 1832, travellers were being encouraged to leave the road and enjoy the scenery from a purpose-built lookout at Wentworth Falls. Temperate rainforest (opposite) thrives in the moist conditions around the waterfalls of Valley of Waters Creek below the Conservation Hut.

With some way still to go, Mathias Steinberg (right) climbs the steps from the National Pass. Although the base of the cliff is about 200 m from the summit at this point, the floor of the Jamison Valley is a further 200 m or so below. At the top of his climb, Mathias will reach the pool at Queens Cascade (below), from which Jamison Creek pours over the first of the two cataracts of Wentworth Falls. The fine spray that covers the cliffs around Wentworth Falls (opposite) creates the moist environment in which the rare dwarf pine thrives. Only about 300 specimens of this plant remain, and they are found only here. They are a relic of the time when Australia was part of the supercontinent Gondwana, from which it finally split about 45 million years ago.

TRAVEL ADVICE

3801 Limited runs regular day tours from Sydney to the Blue Mountains and other areas. Write to 3801 Limited, PO Box 3801, Redfern, NSW 2016, ☎ 1300 65 3801.

For information about national parks facilities and ranger-guided activities around Glenbrook, contact the NPWS at the Heritage Centre in Blackheath (see p. 41).

The Blue Mountains Tourism Authority has an information centre and shop, open daily, on the Great Western Highway at Glenbrook. ☎ 1300 65 3408, <www.bluemts.com.au>.

The Norman Lindsay Gallery is at 128 Chapman Parade, Faulconbridge, ☎ 02 4751 1067. The gallery is open daily – 10 a.m.–4 p.m.

The Woodford Academy is on the Great Western Highway at Woodford. Normally open once monthly, but special tours can be arranged for parties of 20 or more. Write to PO Box 23, Woodford, NSW 2778, ☎ 02 4759 2647 (after hours), <www.nsw.nationaltrust.org.au/wood.html>.

The Falls Gallery is at 161 Falls Road, Wentworth Falls, ☎ 02 4757 1139, <www.bluemts.com.au/Falls Gallery>. It is open 10 a.m.–5 p.m. Wednesday–Sunday and public holidays.

The NPWS Conservation Hut is at the western end of Fletcher Street, Wentworth Falls, ☎ 02 4757 3827. It serves affordable light meals and has a shop.

The smile of a steam buff. Warren Lloyd in the hot seat of steam locomotive 3830 as it climbs the eastern escarpment of the Blue Mountains on the way to Glenbrook.

sandstone – that runs for about 3 km along the middle of the cliff face. Steps cut into the rock at steep inclines, and railings installed in exposed parts, are reminders of the dangers that the track makers faced.

As I topped the first carved steps from Valley of Waters Creek, I saw the track winding ahead and the cliffs receding towards Kings Tableland. From here on I walked with such a view on my right-hand side that sometimes I felt I was flying. Bellbirds clinked far below, and now and then I detoured behind showers falling from hanging swamps or heathlands on the clifftops high above me. Halfway along the track I walked behind the spray of the Den Fenella waterfall as it plunged down the tube it has carved in the cliff.

The waterfall at Wentworth Falls is said to be among the most beautiful in the mountains. I certainly agreed with that assertion as I climbed past its various levels, cascades and pools at the end of my walk. I felt smug, too, about having seen them from more perspectives than the illustrious naturalist. But then he didn't have the benefit of more than 100 years of track-building behind him.

City in the mountains

Historic settlement of crags and vistas

Tall and striking, with a wild frizz of black hair, Trish Follenfant is unashamedly passionate about the garden that is her workplace. "I hate weekends because I'm not here," she said.

We were standing with our backs to a wall. On the other side of the wall was wilderness untamed: the Jamison Valley, receding in shades of blue towards Mount Solitary. In front of us, wilderness tamed: a long rectangular lawn urged the eye towards a cream-coloured building with generous windows.

The lawn was on one of several terraces, retained by exquisitely made dry-stone walls, that had been hacked by hand into a sloping 5 ha block on the edge of Gordon Creek gully. The building – once a squash court and now home to an art gallery – and terraces belonged to Everglades Gardens in Leura, the next township up the line from Wentworth Falls.

Everglades, administered by the National Trust and one of the few Blue Mountains gardens that encourages visitors year round, dates from 1933 when landscape designer Paul Sorensen created them for floor-covering tycoon Henri Van de Velde. Trained in horticulture in his native Denmark, Sorensen designed the gardens of Katoomba's Carrington Hotel and several estates

before he met Van de Velde. Sorensen believed the dramatic view from the Everglades site would swamp the gardens if allowed to, so he designed them in such a way that, when you walk through them, the view appears in discrete tableaus.

Trish, manager of Everglades for the past five years, showed me through the gardens and the two Art Deco buildings that Van de Velde built to Sorensen's design. "Sorensen loved to create spaces. He wanted to surprise; everywhere in the gardens you'll find little nooks and hidden features," she said.

The railway made possible the creation of impressive gardens and homes in the Blue Mountains; much more than Cox's road, it opened the region to development and tourism.

From Weatherboard (Wentworth Falls), the line was extended in 1869 to Mount Victoria, which became the terminus while Whitton's Great Zig Zag was built. The first train to make the complete crossing of the mountains arrived at Bowenfels (now in Lithgow) in 1869. The link to Bathurst was completed in 1876. This new accessibility to the mountains was highlighted when Prince Alfred, Duke of Edinburgh, made a much-publicised rail excursion to Weatherboard in 1868.

Paragon of good taste. Katoomba's Paragon café-restaurant has a richly deserved reputation for the excellence of its hand-made confectionery. Established by Zacharias Simos in 1916, the Paragon has been classified by the National Trust. It has a sumptuous Art Deco interior, complete with solid maple wall panelling and scenes from classical Greek mythology depicted in alabaster on the wood.

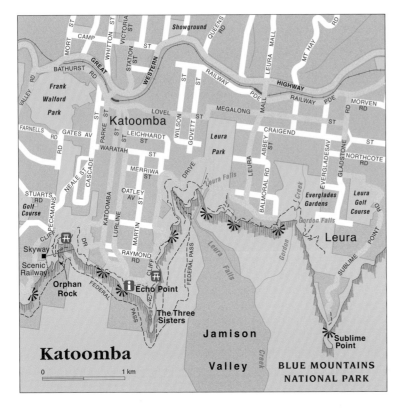

An artfully devised pergola (above right) frames Mount Solitary and the wilderness of the southern Blue Mountains. Landscape designer Paul Sorensen deliberately used such devices to prevent the wilderness from overwhelming Everglades, the gardens he created in Leura in the 1930s. Everglades, owned and managed by The National Trust of Australia (NSW), can be hired for functions and musical performances. Guests (right) at a 21st birthday party in the gardens chat in a fern bower. Stunning views of the Blue Mountains open up from the upper windows of Leura House (opposite above), a guesthouse dating from the 1880s and managed by co-owner John Ekin, pictured on the balcony above the colonnade of the building's western facade. (Opposite below) With mountain vistas like these around them, golfers on Leura Golf Course have a hard time keeping their eye on the ball.

Sydney's wealthy were now able to build large country retreats (some with their own private railway sidings) along the line, and many commuted from the mountains to the city. The railway also brought trippers keen to enjoy the natural wonders in Sydney's backyard. Soon a range of accommodation, restaurants and their ancillary industries sprang up and the settlements began superficially to take on the look of English country towns.

Growth along the line was phenomenal. By 1908 Katoomba had a permanent population of 3500. Six years later it had doubled. And to keep the tourists coming, little time was lost in developing facilities and attractions, such as lookouts and walking tracks. By the 1920s, growing numbers of motorists encouraged the building of scenic drives (resulting in the neglect of the walking tracks).

While luxury hotels looked after the smart set, guesthouses catered for middle- and working-class visitors. The guesthouse era peaked in the late 1920s, when well over 100 guesthouses (90 in Katoomba alone) dotted the mountains. One of the finest was Leura House, an elaborate Italianate mansion built in the 1880s on a prominence above the railway line and road in Leura.

"Leura House was an extremely popular guesthouse in its day," said John Ekin, its laconic manager and one of its current owners. "Leura was small and pretty and this was obviously built to try to develop the village. It was never intended to compete with the Carrington Hotel in Katoomba, which in its day was considered the best hotel in Australia. The Carrington was large and luxurious, whereas this was small but comfortable and grandly domestic."

Like Blue Mountains tourism generally, Leura House's fortunes declined after World War II. In 1950 the Daughters of Our Lady of the Sacred Heart took it over and used it to accommodate nuns-in-training. John and partner Mario Romilio bought it in 1980 and restored the building to its former grandeur, reopening it as a guesthouse in 1990.

Leura has an air of quiet sophistication that exudes from the neat shops and galleries. In the streets around the mall you'll find elegantly restored houses, many of which can be rented by visitors. Maurice Cooper, a self-confessed hoarder of absolutely everything, runs Bygone Beautys, an antique shop cum tea-room on Grose Street. With partner Ron Hooper, he owns restored cottages, in Leura and neighbouring townships, that he rents to visitors.

"Leura is old wealth," Maurice said. But things are changing. "Wentworth Falls is new wealth, and Blackheath is coming up rapidly."

LEURA MAY BE what Wentworth Falls and Blackheath are aspiring to be but what Katoomba has apparently decided not to be. Katoomba is only a 20-minute walk or a five-minute train ride from Leura but far removed from it in style. This struck me the moment I turned into its main shopping thoroughfare, Katoomba Street, near the station.

The luxurious Fairmont Resort (opposite) and Leura Golf Course dominate the clifftop between Inspiration Point and Sublime Point, on Leura's eastern side. Below the headlands spreads the Jamison Valley, with Mount Solitary on its far side in the middle distance. The Three Sisters can be seen on the next headland to the west of Sublime Point, on the upper right of the picture. Mount Solitary (above) glowers over the Jamison Valley in this view from Narrow Neck Plateau. On the left is Malaita Point, where one night in 1931 a cliff collapsed unheard as a result of coalmining beneath it. With its smart restaurants, galleries and antique shops, The Mall, Leura (left), caters for visitors searching for style.

With its population of nearly 9000, Katoomba is the biggest town in the Blue Mountains and the region's capital. From here the 26 townships and villages strung along the 60 km urban strip – with a total population of nearly 74,000 and collectively known as the City of the Blue Mountains – are administered by a single local government body, the Blue Mountains City Council. Two hours and 122 km from Sydney, the town hosts more than 2 million visitors a year (compared with 500,000 in 1928), most of whom arrive by car or bus. Tourism, employing 4750 people directly and an unquantifiable but large segment of the population indirectly, is the area's only significant industry, making it particularly vulnerable to economic fluctuations in other parts of Australia and overseas.

Ever since the families of miners rubbed shoulders with the well-to-do in the late 1800s, Katoomba has been a brash fusion of upmarket and downmarket. On the day I was there, a bitter wind was hurling clouds from the south. Shoppers sheltered in fuggy cafés as occasional snow flurries swirled under shop awnings. Katoomba Street dropped in a straight line to where the city came to a precipitous end at the Jamison Valley 2.5 km from the station. That now familiar edge. The view was sharp as ice crystals under the lowering sky. Beyond the edge, beyond the valley and Mount Solitary, I could see for 50 km across the steel-grey expanse of Kanangra-Boyd and Blue Mountains national parks to the south. I made my way to the bottom of Katoomba

Dwarfed by the immensity of the mountain landscape (opposite left), tourists venture across a steel bridge to the first of the Three Sisters, having descended part of the Giant Stairway from Katoomba's Echo Point. Legend suggests that the pinnacles are named after the three daughters of an Aboriginal cleverman who turned them to stone to protect them from a bunyip. Like all the townships that make up the City of the Blue Mountains, Katoomba (opposite right), largest of the mountain centres, sits on the very edge of a timeless wilderness. The region's attraction for many visitors, such as these (above) at Echo Point, is the thrill of looking over the edge without having to forsake the comforts of civilisation.

Street, where I turned left for Echo Point, one of NSW's most popular tourist sites and the hub around which the Blue Mountains revolves.

So many people come here to stare from its lookouts into the depths of the Jamison Valley and at the triple rock spires known as the Three Sisters that in 1998 the council feared the spot was being "loved to death". It estimated that 5800 buses and cars visited the spot daily during peak periods. In January 1999, the State Government pledged to give Katoomba a $13 million facelift. About $8 million would go on roadworks, walls, stairs, bush regeneration and a new viewing deck at Echo Point.

And the scene on the day I was there certainly highlighted the necessity of protecting Echo Point. The buses and cars came and went; the people crowded the lookouts. A few tackled the steps down to the first of the Three Sisters; fewer still kept on going down the Giant Stairway to the Dardanelles and Federal passes. A woman behind the counter in the tourist information centre near the lookouts said it had been a busy winter. "Every time there's mention of snow the people come rushing up from Sydney."

I took the Prince Henry Cliff Walk westwards to the Scenic Railway. Here, beside Orphan Rock, on the edge of one of the planet's most stunning natural panoramas, brashness reaches its zenith.

The Scenic Railway is the most cheerfully in-your-face facility imaginable, with a fairground atmosphere that overwhelms the senses from the moment you confront the concrete statue of the legendary Three Sisters near the main entrance. A disused roller-coaster track careens overhead. Buses arriving to disgorge tourists drive right under the pulley system of the facility's other major attraction, the Scenic Skyway. The cluster of rectangular buildings includes a cinema, a revolving restaurant and an enormous souvenir shop.

With a gradient of 55 per cent (229 m in 415 m), the Scenic Railway was originally used for lifting coal and kerosene shale from mines in the Jamison and Megalong valleys. Katoomba Colliery Ltd, which ran it from 1925, would allow walkers to hitch lifts in the coal skip. As this became an increasingly popular means of getting from the bottom of the valley, the company built a series of ever-better passenger skips and, in 1933, opened a facility called the Katoomba Colliery Scenic Railway. The railway's popularity notwithstanding, Katoomba Colliery Ltd went broke at the end of WWII. When it came on the market in 1945, there was only one tender – from Harry Hammon, a Katoomba haulage contractor, and Isobel, his sister and business partner.

"Dad had no idea what the scenic railway was going to become," Harry's son, Phil, told me. I remarked on the earthy, fairground atmosphere of the clifftop facilities Phil laughed. "It's unique. There's nothing like it anywhere," he said.

He's got 1.2 million customers a year to second that. Like any good fairground, Phil's complex offers heart-stopping thrills that make you feel tinglingly alive when you walk away from them. Compared with the Scenic Railway, the Skyway offers a less-concentrated buzz; even so, 300,000 people a year are happy to take the seven-minute ride in the cable car 300 m above a rainforested gorge.

The Scenic Railway (opposite), beside Orphan Rock, offers a knee-trembling ride as it plunges into the Jamison Valley. Formerly used to lift coal and kerosene shale from mines in the valley, the railway descends 229 m vertically in its 415 m journey, passing through a tunnel to shady rainforest. It is the world's steepest inclined funicular railway and carries 84 people at a time, making the trip every 10 minutes, from 9 a.m. to 4.50 p.m. 365 days a year. The Scenic Skyway (below) is the other major attraction of the Scenic Railway complex. It pauses 300 m above the gorge of Katoomba Falls creek for a few minutes to allow its 30 passengers to take in the view and listen to the sounds of the rainforest – the swish of cascading water, the song of superb lyrebirds, pied currawongs and eastern whipbirds – drifting up from below. The journey takes 7 minutes.

HIGH ADVENTURE, HIGH IMPACT

The Blue Mountains are synonymous with adventure. They attract bushwalkers, rockclimbers, canyoners, abseilers and mountain-bikers. There is horseriding on the edges of the national parks, and many bushwalkers become anglers when they reach a river. Visitors have been tramping through the mountains since the mid-1800s, rockclimbing since at least the 1930s and canyoning since the 1940s.

According to Derek Murphy, a director and instructor with Katoomba's Australian School of Mountaineering, more than 10,000 people a year rockclimb in the Blue Mountains and up to three times that number abseil, mostly in canyons. And that's the problem. These three sports have become so popular that they are harming the places where they are practised. The NPWS says adverse impacts include damage to rock and vegetation, erosion, creation of tracks and placement of anchor bolts in rock.

By 1998, some 500 people were climbing the Three Sisters annually. As a result of damage to the site, the NPWS was intending, at the time of writing, to put a temporary ban on abseiling and rockclimbing there to allow for rehabilitation. The service said the degradation was "inconsistent with … the feature's status as an internationally recognised natural icon and tourist attraction". Several other sites have been closed to abseiling and climbing activities.

The NPWS calculates that the Blue Mountains NP gets nearly 2 million visitors a year and expects this figure to jump by 40 per cent in the next five years. Not surprisingly, it is considering further bans and restrictions on adventure sports, particularly where large groups are concerned.

Derek backs some of these measures. "We are working in consultation with the NPWS to establish a plan of management. The NPWS are setting the agenda and we are helping them."

Awash in icy water (above), adventurer Sue Wilson negotiates Hole-in-the-Wall Canyon, near the border between Wollemi National Park and Newnes State Forest. This canyon, which is graded 4 (moderate to difficult) on the canyon rating scale, features a narrow squeeze through a dark cleft – definitely not for large people! The cleft is spectacularly lit by glow worms. Andrew McCauley (opposite) leads the fifth pitch on a route known as Crash Test Dummies at Pierces Pass, in the Grose Valley. Although individuals had climbed rock faces in the Blue Mountains as far back as the early 1800s, it was only in 1929 that climbers formed a club. Called the Katoomba Suicide Club, it was probably the first rockclimbing organisation in Australia. Its founder was Eric Dark, a doctor, and one of its members was his wife Eleanor, the historical novelist renowned for her trilogy THE TIMELESS LAND.

KATOOMBA AND THE CARRINGTON

Until the railway came through in 1868, Katoomba consisted of an inn on Pulpit Hill, 2 km west of today's station. From 1871, the locality was called The Crushers, after a stone quarry beside the railway line. A platform was built in 1874. The settlement's fortunes improved after John North opened a coalmine below Orphan Rock in 1879. The previous year, the settlement had also acquired a new name, Katoomba – reportedly from an Aboriginal word *kedumba*, meaning "falling water".

Although other Blue Mountains settlements had been popular for country retreats in the 1870s, Katoomba did not become fashionable until the 1880s and 1890s. The transformation was sparked in 1882 by the building of the 60-room Great Western Hotel, originally intended for Wentworth Falls, high on a hill above the station. Four years later it was extended and renamed the Carrington, after the then NSW Governor, Charles Wynn-Carrington, who often stayed there.

HARRY PHILLIPS/COURTESY: BLUE MOUNTAINS HISTORICAL SOCIETY

By 1905 the Carrington was being referred to as "the largest and best-known tourist hotel in the Southern Hemisphere". Adventurer and newspaper magnate Sir James Joynton-Smith, who already owned the Imperial Hotel in Mount Victoria, bought it in 1911 and added the powerhouse and the octagonal chimney stack. Until 1925, the hotel supplied electricity to Katoomba and villages between Mount Victoria and Woodford. Joynton-Smith also added the magnificent Italianate balcony. In 1927 a further wing was built, bringing the total number of rooms to 200.

Katoomba and the Carrington both suffered during the post-war decline in mountain tourism. The hotel was closed from 1985 until Geoff Leach bought it in 1991. The city's elders saw the hotel's restoration and its reopening late in 1998 as the start of Katoomba's rejuvenation. "We want it alive and kicking like it was in the halcyon days," one said.

The leadlight windows (above) on the refurbished Carrington's front veranda come spectacularly to life at night. From the time it was opened in 1882, the hotel dominated Katoomba's skyline. When this photograph (left) was shot in 1915, the gardens were well established.

The writer's craft (left). Peter Bishop, executive director of VARUNA, a residential retreat for writers, helps visiting wordsmith Lyndel Caffrey with her text. Writers can stay at the centre for three weeks at a time and work on projects of their choice. "We target new writers who have not been published and they work here with other writers," Peter said. The centrepiece of the Hydro Majestic Hotel (below), at Medlow Bath, is the domed casino (entertainment room). Businessman Mark Foy, the hotel's creator, imported the domed, pressed-metal roof of the casino's ballroom from Chicago in 1903.

A few blocks away is a facility at the other end of the cultural spectrum. The fact that it gets a few hundred visitors a year compared with the Scenic Railway's million-plus was food for thought as I walked to it.

Varuna, at 141 Cascade Street, was formerly the home and workplace of author Eleanor Dark, best known for her historical trilogy *The Timeless Land*. Now it is the headquarters of the Eleanor Dark Foundation, which runs *Varuna* as a residential retreat for visiting writers. "There are lots of writers' centres but we're the only residential one in Australia and the only national one," Peter Bishop, the centre's executive director, told me. "We run 24 three-week fellowships every year for writers from all over Australia. We get 24 writers, four at a time, coming here to work on projects. Each has a bedroom and private space."

Peter, 46, with heavy spectacles and a greying beard, has a youthfully studious air and an intensity behind his soft-spoken manner. He said that, on top of the fellowships, the centre organises a number of other programs and courses for writers and puts on 40 or more events a year, including book launches and readings.

"A lot of books have come out of all this, and a lot of writers, having come here, have decided the Blue Mountains is a great place to live," Peter said.

That has long been the case. The list of literary residents includes poet Harry Peckman, Dymphna Cusack, Kylie Tennant, Gabrielle Lord and David Foster. With local artists, they have contributed to the perception of the region as a thriving cultural centre, a view that the NSW Government formalised by declaring the Blue Mountains its inaugural City of the Arts in 1995.

YOU CAN PINPOINT KATOOMBA from anywhere in the mountains by its chimney stack, but few visitors know that the chimney was once part of a private powerhouse attached to the Carrington Hotel.

Even though, at the time of my visit, the Carrington had slipped into dereliction and ceased to be a social focal point, it still dominated Katoomba physically, both as the town's largest structure and through its hilltop position. On my walk from *Varuna* back to the station, I was delighted to notice that the venerable building, looking like the bridge of a vast ocean liner, was having some work done on it. Just how comprehensive the work actually was I discovered after I knocked on the Art Nouveau, leadlight front door. It was opened by Geoff Leach, one of the four owners.

Tall and with film-star good looks, Geoff explained that he had bought the Carrington for $2 million in 1991 because he hated to see such a beautiful building going to ruin. As a builder, he said, he derived his greatest pleasure not so much from ownership of the 1882 hotel but from returning it to its original splendour.

"I came up here 20 years ago to play in some golf tournaments and stayed at the Carrington. It was a fabulous place," Geoff said. "I love old buildings; they have so much more charm and character than modern ones."

Geoff showed me the work in progress. The task seemed monumental, and it did not surprise me to hear that the refurbishment was going to cost $3 million. And that, he said, was cheap because he was doing much of the work himself.

"This was very derelict. There was lots of water damage. We've been drying the building out for years," he said. "We're restoring it to the way it was in the early 1900s, right down to the carpets."

Restoration was in the air, it seemed. One stop up the railway line, at the tiny village of Medlow Bath, I discovered that the Hydro Majestic Hotel, once a fashionable resort for Sydney high society, was also being returned to its former glory.

Standing across the Great Western Highway from the railway station, the hotel sprawls 300 m along the edge of a cliff overlooking the Megalong Valley. The white and apricot complex of buildings is an eye-catching farrago of styles from different eras, starting in the late 1800s. The Hydro opened as the Hydropathic Sanatorium on 4 July 1904 in the middle of a snowstorm during which the state-of-the-art electricity supply system failed, forcing the 200 guests at the opening ceremony to huddle in overcoats and blankets for the official photograph.

Coincidentally, isolated snowflakes were falling from a charcoal-grey sky when I arrived. The Hydro's historian, Paul Innes, who doubled as Santa for the hotel's weekly Yulefest celebrations in winter, showed me through the labyrinth of rooms and passages, some already restored and in use.

The palatial resort was the brainchild of department store magnate Mark Foy, who had been cured of indigestion at Matlock, an English spa town. Impressed, he dreamt of creating something similar in Australia.

Foy bought an existing hotel on the site and amalgamated it with a number of other buildings by means of long corridors, adding a casino (an entertainment room rather than a gambling venue) topped by an elaborate pressed-metal dome imported from Chicago in 1903. The resort was Australia's longest building at the time.

Lavishly furnishing the interior, Foy installed a range of the most up-to-date hydropathic devices, including douches, multi-rosed showers, mudbaths and hip baths. He imported spa water from Baden Baden, in Germany, and provided a light-bath – in which visitors could enjoy the supposedly therapeutic properties of electric light. However, the sanatorium and its austere treatments proved unpopular and after 18 months Foy dismissed the doctors and abandoned the water treatments.

Renamed the Hydro Majestic, the resort was a huge success and, despite a fire that destroyed half the building in 1922, it continued to attract visitors, both from Australia and overseas, through the Depression and two world wars. By the 1990s

The Hydro Majestic's western windows (opposite above) offer a panorama of the Megalong Valley. In the hotel's early days, much of its food was grown on a farm in the valley and was hoisted up by flying fox, the ruins of which can still be seen. In the late 1990s the hotel, which had begun to show its age, was being refurbished (opposite below) and refurnished in its original Art Nouveau and Art Deco styles in a bid to recapture the magic of its heyday, the 1920s and '30s. Guests enjoying a meal in the Casino Lounge (below) can savour stunning views over the valley's rolling farmland to the Great Dividing Range in the west and Kanangra-Boyd National Park in the south.

A shaft of sunlight (right) picks out walker Ursula Känel in the Grand Canyon, near Blackheath. Here sandstone walls towering 100 metres above the gorge floor help keep the atmosphere cool and moist. Moderately fit walkers without specialised equipment can experience part of the Grand Canyon in a circular trip that takes 3–4 hours. Sunrise (below) sets the rocks ablaze on a headland overlooking Govett Gorge. A walking track linking Govetts Leap, Evans Lookout and the Grand Canyon passes just behind the cliff.

it had acquired some unsympathetic additions and was showing its age. At the time of my visit, the Peppers Group had the refurbishment and management contract on it, with work due to be finished in 1999.

I suspect that one of the most curative pastimes Hydro guests could indulge in was to contemplate the stupendous view from its west-facing windows across the Megalong Valley and the valley of the Coxs River to the Great Dividing Range. Undoubtedly another was walking on the 20 km of tracks in the bush below the hotel.

I ARRIVED IN BLACKHEATH, the neighbouring village, in a near-blizzard. I had an appointment with Ian Brown, the NPWS district operations manager, at the service's Blue Mountains headquarters in the Heritage Centre on Govetts Leap Road. I set out to walk there, but after a few blocks I wondered if I'd made the right decision.

The wind thundered in the trees, blowing snow horizontally across the road and plastering it against tree trunks. In some places the spindrift was so thick I could not see my feet. Here and there extravagant colour lit the sombre scene: the gold of wattles in flower and the brilliant red of crimson rosellas feeding on a snow-covered lawn. At one point I had to detour around a large gum tree that had fallen across the road. I'd never seen the Blue Mountains like this.

William Govett was probably the first European to admire the view from Govetts Leap lookout across Govett Gorge when he surveyed the area in 1831. Partly for fun and partly to gauge the height of the cliff, he pushed boulders over the edge and timed their fall. He concluded (reasonably correctly) that the cliff was 160 m high and the floor of the valley about 600 m deep. Bridal Veil Falls, halfway along the cliff on the right, are among the highest single-drop falls in the Blue Mountains.

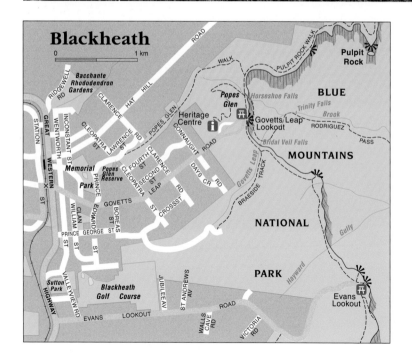

Launching (top) from 1076 m high Mount Blackheath, 4 km as the crow flies from Blackheath village, a hang glider heads out over the Kanimbla Valley. Hang gliders take off from a purpose-built ramp near the mountain's lookout and may reach Bathurst, 70 km to the west. Govetts Leap lookout (above) attracts almost as many sightseers as Echo Point.

Despite the weather, I made it to my appointment punctually. While Ian and I were talking, the power failed. But though the wind continued to blow, the sun had come out by the time we'd finished. It was wild, exhilarating weather. I decided to take the short (less than 1 km) but pretty Fairfax Heritage Track from the Heritage Centre to Govetts Leap. The wattle blossom glowed against the white background, which was already beginning to melt in the strengthening sunlight. By the time I reached Govetts Leap the trees were shedding water like rain.

You never get accustomed to the views in the Blue Mountains. They may have the same ingredients but each is unique. So it was with the 600 m deep Grose Gorge beneath the lookouts at Govetts Leap. Unlike the valleys I'd seen recently, such as the Jamison and the Megalong, this was a good deal narrower and more formidable looking. Contemplating the chasm that in 1836 Darwin had described as "stupendous" and explorer Paul de Strzelecki in 1839 as "narrow, gloomy and profound", I decided to make it my next destination. It was time to step off the edge into eternity again.

I returned to Blackheath via the 2 km Braeside Walk, created in the 1930s for motorised visitors looking for short walks from car parks. Back in the village, I grabbed a meal in a warm café before my train. Renowned for its rhododendron festival in early November, its many walks (from short and easy to long and hard), some well-restored guesthouses and a number of quality eating places, Blackheath was fast becoming a popular destination in the mountains.

The westernmost Blue Mountains settlement on the Great Western Highway and railway line is Mount Victoria. This tiny village, at the highest point (1094 m) in the central Blue Mountains, boasts several historic hotels and guesthouses, including the pink, castellated Imperial Hotel. The Imperial dates from 1878 and was owned by Sir James Joynton-Smith before he bought the Carrington in Katoomba.

If you're travelling by car, you have a choice of routes from here. You can keep going on the highway to Lithgow, passing Mount York on your right (where you can still see remnants of Cox's original road) and descending via Victoria Pass to

Overhung by a mass of sandstone, a zigzag track takes Denise Fuchs down towards the base of Bridal Veil Falls, in Govetts Gorge. Many cliffs in the Blue Mountains are topped with hanging swamps. These occur where a layer of impermeable claystone covers the permeable sandstone. They act like giant sponges, soaking up water that flows from woodlands above and releasing it in the form of permanent creeks. The swamps provide an important refuge for animals and insects, among them the Blue Mountains water skink, found only in the region.

Dubbed "Whitton's Masterpiece" after its designer, John Whitton, engineer-in-chief of NSW Railways, the Great Zig Zag (above) was begun in 1866 and took 700 men over three years to blast and hack out of the rocky escarpment. In places surveyors had to dangle from ropes while pegging out the route. The layout of the zigzag, with its system of elevated viaducts, can be seen in the picture opposite. The viaduct in the foreground obscures the middle viaduct.

historic Hartley and the Coxs River. Or you can go north along the Darling Causeway to Bells Line of Road. This is the route followed by the railway line, and since I was travelling by train, I had no choice. Besides, I wanted to end my journey across the mountains as I'd begun it – on a steam train.

At Zig Zag, the last station before Lithgow, the train stops to pick up or set down passengers on request. It is a quaint touch. The only reason for getting off here is to ride on Whitton's Great Zig Zag.

The zigzag line travels about 8 km over three beautiful sandstone viaducts and through two tunnels in its 210 m descent. As on the eastern zigzag, it doubles back on itself at two sets of points to create a flattened Z. And like the eastern zigzag, it was superseded (in 1910) by a deviation that cut travel time to Lithgow by 30 minutes.

Today the Zig Zag Railway Co-op Ltd runs vintage trains up and down the zigzag for the benefit of tourists. The return journey by steam train takes about an hour and a half. As I stood on the platform at Zig Zag, steam from the Class DD 17 loco No. 1049 swirling about my legs, black coal smoke blotting out the sun above me and soot smuts settling in my hair, I couldn't help feeling that, with the passing of the steam age, the Blue Mountains lost just a little of their magic.

TRAVEL ADVICE

Everglades Gardens, 37 Everglades Avenue, Leura, are open daily 10 a.m.–5 p.m. in spring and summer and to 4 p.m. in autumn and winter. Admission fees are modest. There is a gift shop, and teas and snacks are available. ☎ 02 4784 1938, <www.nsw.nationaltrust.org.au/ever.html>.

Leura House, 7 Britain Street, Leura, offers a range of accommodation styles and packages, including Yulefest weekends. ☎ 02 4784 2035.

Bygone Beautys has fully equipped accommodation, from Victorian weekenders and Edwardian cottages to modern duplexes. Contact Bygone Beautys Shop and Tearoom, 20–22 Grose Street, Leura, NSW 2780, ☎ 02 4783 3117. There is a Bygone Beautys Shop at 122 Main Street, Katoomba.

The huge range of adventure activities available in the Blue Mountains is catered for by too many groups and organisations to list here. Initial contact can be made through the Blue Mountains Tourism Authority. The information centre and shop at Echo Point is open daily (see p. 87).

The Scenic Railway and Skyway, off Cliff Drive, Katoomba, are open daily 9 a.m.–5 p.m. throughout the year. ☎ 02 4782 2699.

Varuna supports Australian literature and fosters contact between writers and the community. For information on membership and events, ☎ 02 4782 5674 or email <varuna@ozemail.com.au>.

The Carrington Hotel is between Katoomba Street and Parke Street, ☎ 02 4782 1111. The Hydro Majestic, at Medlow Bath, can be contacted on ☎ 02 4788 1002, and the Imperial Hotel at Mount Victoria on ☎ 02 4787 1233.

The Zig Zag Railway, off Bells Line of Road at Clarence (between Bell and Lithgow), runs steam trains on weekends, public holidays and during most of the NSW public school holidays. At other times a vintage rail motor does the trip. For information on timetables and membership, ☎ 02 6353 1795 during business hours or 02 6351 4826 for a recorded message.

Wild depths, horticultural heights

The Grose Valley

An eruption of fiery autumn colours lights up Mount Tomah Botanic Garden, on Bells Line of Road, as the leaves of its many exotic shrubs and trees die and fall. The nutrient-rich volcanic soil of the mountain that gives the garden its name encourages lush growth, and many species brought from overseas grow larger here than in their natural environment.

Fairy Grotto seemed just the sort of place to run into all manner of mythical creatures. A limpid creek poured over boulders from one pool to another, past tiny moss gardens, under arches of fern fronds, beside miniature sandy beaches. The air was cool and moist, the sky unseen somewhere above a dense canopy of sassafras and lilly pilly.

Don Fuchs and I had reached this pocket of rainforest soon after beginning our descent into the Grose Gorge from its northern rim. Having left our vehicle in the car park at the end of Pierces Pass road (off Bells Line of Road) and shouldered our backpacks, we were descending what used to be called the Hungerford Track but is now Pierces Pass. We'd started in open eucalypt woodland but quickly found ourselves in this dark dell on Pierces Creek. On a hot day we would have welcomed the coolness, but this was August and it looked like rain.

A short distance beyond the grotto, the rainforest abruptly gave way to open woodland, offering views of high cliffs with angular faults to our right. Minutes later, as we emerged from the pass and began zigzagging down into the gorge, we had a magnificent view across to the southern side, to Burramoko Head and its most striking feature, the precarious cliff known as Hanging Rock. Great

walls in shades of gold surrounded us, and far below we could hear the Grose River.

Chert flakes found near the track indicate that Pierces Pass was almost certainly used by Aboriginals before Europeans. It was evidently one of several access points into the gorge, some flagged by stone arrangements, art sites and sharpening grooves.

The Grose Gorge is bounded on the north and south by the ridges that carry the Great Western Highway and Bells Line of Road and on the west by the Darling Causeway. The Grose River rises beneath the causeway and, for the first 20–30 km of its eastward descent, where it is known as the Upper Grose, it has carved out a relatively wide gorge through soft shale and mudstone. This was the part we were entering.

Due south of Mount Tomah, the Lower Grose strikes harder sandstone, and there it vanishes into slot-like canyons and stepped, boulder-strewn gorges up to 400 m deep, beginning at the Kolonga Canyon. Below this, the maze of wild, secret depths is so forbidding that it has attracted names like Kolonga Labyrinth (reportedly from the Aboriginal word *kolonga*, meaning "out of the way place") and The Devils Wilderness. The Confederation of

Definitely not for the faint-hearted (above), these pools on the rim of Govett Gorge provide a cool respite for, from left, Paul "Sharkey" Marlin, Trevor Hamilton and Adam "Rusty" Worsman. They have just completed a 40 m swim and a 6 m abseil in a canyon and are psyching themselves up for the return journey. Claustral Canyon (opposite), further east, offers a bigger challenge. Its most spectacular feature is the Black Hole of Calcutta, which requires three 15 m abseils to negotiate. The shortage of space in which to stand between the abseiling sections gives rise to the canyon's name, "Claustral" deriving from "claustrophobia". More than 300 known canyons carve into the Blue Mountains sandstone, offering a lifetime of discovery to keen and well-prepared adventurers. However, canyoning requires specialised techniques and anyone wanting to explore a canyon should do so with NPWS-licensed guides. The NPWS is worried that pressure of visitors is causing erosion and crowding in the most accessible canyons.

Bushwalking Clubs of NSW has proposed that 50,000 ha around the Grose River be officially declared wilderness under the Wilderness Act, and if ever there was a place that deserved the title "wilderness", this is it.

On the east of the Blue Mountains, the Grose emerges from its gorge to join the Nepean River near Richmond, from where it was seen by European settlers in 1789. The first Europeans to try to explore the region were William Dawes and Watkin Tench, who did so in December that year at Governor Phillip's behest. Like so many after them, they were baffled by the terrain. William Paterson, under orders from Major Francis Grose, commander of the NSW Corps, made an attempt in 1793, George Bass following in 1797 and George Caley in 1804. Although posterity has criticised some early explorers for sticking to rivers, Blue Mountains historian Andy Macqueen maintains that many were well aware that they should follow ridges but had difficulty finding them. "It is the nature of Blue Mountains terrain that it is difficult to navigate along ridges even with a map," Macqueen wrote. "Without a map or knowledge of the country, the region becomes an indecipherable maze."

The first European to walk all 64 km of the Grose was probably Edwin Barton, an engineer looking for a railway route through the mountains in 1858. His expedition was followed by the building of a track, known as the Engineers Track, intended to provide access for survey parties. Little of it remains today.

As the sun sets, the rugged battlements (above) of the Grose Gorge, lying to the north and north-west of Blackheath village, take on the colour of old gold. Mount Banks (1062 m), one of several basalt-capped peaks in the region, dominates the skyline. Explorer George Caley climbed it in 1804 and named it after Sir Joseph Banks, botanist on James Cook's ship, HMS ENDEAVOUR. Hanging Rock (opposite left), near Burramoko Head, juts out like a primitive weapon over the Grose Gorge. German visitor Britta Mentzel (opposite right) sits over empty space near Walls Lookout, on the Grose Gorge's northern side.

The railway plan came to nothing, and though other exploiters followed, their grand schemes – for dams to supply water and electricity to Sydney, for forestry, coalmining, industrial development and cattle grazing – also failed.

Clarrie Hungerford and Bert Pierce, World War I veterans who lived on the Bells Line of Road, made an exploratory trip into the gorge sometime before 1930. They were looking for ways to earn money during the Depression and, impressed by the lushness of the wooded flats at the junction of the Grose River and Govetts Creek, they convinced themselves that the land could yield a profit.

In 1930 they started improving the Aboriginal track down Pierces Pass. In January 1931 Hungerford obtained, for a nominal fee, a lease on 16 ha on the eastern side of the Grose River opposite the Govetts Creek junction. The block, within sight of Govetts Leap, was in what was later called Blue Gum Forest. It is not clear what the two men intended to do on the block, whether they planned to fell the forest to provide grazing for their cattle, harvest the timber or, as some have supposed, grow walnuts. It is not certain that they themselves knew.

Don and I had made Blue Gum Forest, only a 3–4-hour walk from the Pierces Pass car park, our destination. My first impression of the Grose River, when we got down to it, stayed with me till I left. It struck me as far less abused by mankind than

THE GREAT SURVIVOR

The Blue Mountains region has the highest density of eucalypt species in the world. Out of 700 species worldwide, 92 are found in the Blue Mountains. Katoomba's environs, with 65 species, may have the world's greatest concentration.

The reason for this remarkable diversity lies in the corresponding variation in climate and terrain in the Blue Mountains. The climate can vary from arid to subalpine and the soil from very rich to very poor – among the world's poorest. Eucalypts flourish in all these environments. You'll find them in the fertile volcanic loam on the region's basalt-capped mountains and the extremely infertile sandy soils of the dry sandstone plateaus of Wollemi National Park.

The Blue Mountains is one of the most fire-prone regions of the world, and it's hardly surprising that one of the eucalypt's greatest adaptations is its tolerance of fire. In fact, most eucalypts can't survive without fire and have a number of devices to encourage it.

For instance, a eucalypt's leaves are full of highly volatile oils, its bark hangs down in strips from trunk or branches after peeling and the leaves and bark it sheds break down slowly, lying around for long periods to provide fuel.

After being burnt, a eucalypt can resprout from tubers underground and from buds under the bark. Most eucalypts regenerate after fire, when their tough seed pods open and drop seed on the ash-strewn ground.

Because eucalypt leaves are long, narrow and well separated, eucalypt canopies allow up to 50 per cent of sunlight to penetrate, encouraging a dense and variable understorey growth.

Destined eventually to join the Hawkesbury River at Richmond, some 30 km to the east as the crow flies, the Grose River (opposite) cascades noisily through its gorge below Pierces Pass. The river rises below the Darling Causeway and, with its tributaries, is one of the main influences on the shape of the Blue Mountains. In the gorges around the river's higher reaches, the vegetation varies widely, from swamp and fern garden to rainforest and eucalypt woodland. Eucalypts (below) predominate, reaching a climax in Blue Gum Forest, at the junction of the Grose River and Govetts Creek.

the Kowmung, even though it has probably seen more visitors over the years. I saw a few weeds here and there, but not as many as on the Kowmung. And the banks did not have that trampled look but seemed solidly held in place by dense coverings of grasses and ferns.

The further we walked, the more beautiful the river became. Not even increasing cold and rain changed my view. We followed a well-worn track on the southern bank of the river through woodlands of silvertop ash, Sydney peppermint, grey gum, bloodwood and a range of other eucalypts. On the shadier northern slopes of the gorge grew moisture-loving gums such as stringybarks. And blue gums began to catch the eye.

By now the rain was falling heavily and cloud filled the gorge, hiding the cliffs. The blue gums became taller and more numerous as we moved downstream. They had a flayed look; they were shedding their blue-grey bark in long strips, revealing new bark of a pale yellow that glowed through the mist, making their pencil-straight trunks look like vertical strip lights. After about two and a half hours of walking we came to a whole forest of such strip lights, tall and almost flawlessly straight, growing from a meadow of grass and bracken on the south bank of the river, their canopies lost in cloud. This was Little Blue Gum Forest.

Not all the people who visited the Grose in the early years came with exploitation in mind. Some just wanted to experience wilderness for its own sake. Photographers, scientists and even a novelist-journalist, Louisa Atkinson, were among those who explored the river after the Engineers Track was built.

One of the more remarkable ventures was an expedition organised in 1875 by Eccleston du Faur, a businessman and patron of the arts and exploration who had bought land at Mount Wilson that year and who contributed to the early development of the village. Du Faur was obsessed with the Blue Mountains and wanted to publicise their unique beauty. His party, consisting of more than 20 artists, photographers, teachers and a number of other adventurous people (all male), spent three weeks at Blue Gum Forest and left when heavy rain began to fill the Grose.

Following du Faur's expedition, adventurers began to make increasing inroads into the gorge. In the late 1800s walkers were covering the entire length of the river. By the early 1900s, bushwalkers such as Harry Whitehouse and Cecil Webb were performing feats there that today look prodigious. In a single day in 1916 they covered 45 km on a round trip from Blackheath, walking via Perrys Lookdown and Blue Gum Forest and climbing to the summit of 1062 m high Mount Banks (via the Gordon Smith Chimney, a precipitous ravine in the cliffs) before returning by way of Bell. The walk has become a bushwalking legend. In the same year they walked down the river from Blackheath to Richmond in four days.

Don and I pushed on and reached Blue Gum Forest about 90 minutes later. The rain had eased, but the cloud still hung low. Some of the gums were vast, shooting 50 m or more into the greyness, smooth and branchless all the way to where the

canopy burst like a blue-green firework display. A pair of superb fairy-wrens flitted through the understorey of wattle and bracken, and somewhere a lyrebird was going through its repertoire.

Over Easter 1931, a party of Sydney Bush Walkers and Mountain Trails Club members led by Alan Rigby arrived at Blue Gum Forest and, according to Alan, heard a sound that was far less pleasing than a lyrebird's song. Alan was a commercial artist and an amateur photographer and was also a close friend and walking companion of Myles Dunphy. According to Alan, the sound the walkers heard was that of axes striking trees.

What happened next has gone down in the annals of conservation history. Over the ensuing months, the bushwalkers formed the Blue Gum Forest Committee and offered to pay Hungerford £150 (equivalent to about $8000 in the 1990s) if he gave up his lease. On 15 November 1931, the committee arrived at Blue Gum Forest to finalise the deal. They were stunned to see a felled tree, the handiwork of Hungerford and Pierce. Myles Dunphy, the committee's secretary, wrote later that if this was intended to shock the walkers into making a deal, it worked.

The negotiators sat in a semicircle in pouring rain under capes and hats looking, as Myles wrote, like "miserable, wet Indians in the wet foothills on the eastern side of the Andes". Hungerford dropped his price to £130 and a deal was struck.

NICHOLAS BIRKS/WILDLIGHT AUSTRALIA

Growing on fertile sedimentary flats covering about 25 ha, the trees of Blue Gum Forest (above) rise ramrod-straight to heights of 50 m or more. Since 1970, when camping was banned in the forest, and with the eradication of feral horses and cattle, the forest's understorey of grass, fern and wattle (opposite) has sprung back dramatically, helped along by the conservation work of the Friends of Blue Gum Forest, a group of dedicated volunteers. Camping is allowed only at Acacia Flat, 500 m south of the forest beside Govetts Creek. The lush river flats abound with birdlife. Often heard here and throughout the Blue Mountains, but not often seen, the superb lyrebird intersperses simulated bird calls in its own song. It has also been heard imitating frogs, dogs, cats, saws, telephones, camera motor drives and even starter motors. The Grose Gorge is rich in evidence of pre-European occupation, probably by the Darug group, including axe- and spear-sharpening grooves, engravings and campfire remains.

Did Hungerford have clear plans for the land? It is more probable that he had seen his chance to make a quick quid out of some starry-eyed walkers. Neither is it clear whether the deal actually saved the trees. If Hungerford had kept the lease he might not have felled them. With the rest of the Grose Valley, the forest was destined to be incorporated in the Blue Mountains NP in 1959 anyway, whoever owned the lease. More than anything, the impact of the fight to save the forest was symbolic. It showed conservationists that, given the will, individuals and small groups could do something practical to preserve Australia's primitive areas.

Don and I spent a wet night at Acacia Flat, the camping area on Govetts Creek near Blue Gum Forest. It was still pouring next morning when, not long after we'd packed up our tents, we heard a cooee from back up the track. Don looked at me and conceded defeat: I'd made an arrangement to rendezvous here with Alan Rigby's son Jeff on that morning and Don had bet that the rain would put Jeff off.

We found Jeff, 50, where the track from Perrys Lookdown meets the Grose River track. He had small round spectacles, a scraggly beard and a self-effacing smile. Wearing a droopy bush hat and a rainjacket that completely covered his shorts, he didn't look the kind of bushwalker who would be deterred by rain. An artist and art teacher by profession, Jeff lives in the Blue Mountains village of Bullaburra and has been coming to Blue Gum since the age of 10, though he last camped here 15 years ago. The first thing he said was that he was astonished at how the understorey had grown.

"It used to look like a formal park," Jeff said. "You could see for hundreds of yards. Still, I think it has to be like this, otherwise in 100 years there'll be no forest."

Since camping was banned in Blue Gum Forest in 1970 and the NPWS began to eradicate cattle and horses from the area, the understorey has sprung back.

We waded across the Grose to Hungerford's former lease, where Jeff and his father used to camp on grass but where young gums and wattles now stood shoulder-high. Here we talked about Alan's version of the events on that Easter in 1931.

"Dad told me clearly that they heard people chopping trees. The walkers asked the axemen what the heck they were doing, and the men said they owned the lease and were going to take out all the trees and plant walnuts," Jeff said.

Artist, art teacher and bushwalker Jeff Rigby admires a venerable blue gum in Blue Gum Forest, which he has been visiting since he was 10 years old. In 1931 Jeff's father, Alan, was outraged when he discovered that the forest's trees were about to be felled. Alan persuaded fellow bushwalkers to form the Blue Gum Forest Committee, which raised enough money to pay the leaseholder to forfeit his lease. In 1932 the NSW Lands Department made the forest a reserve.

"They may well have spun Dad a line about the walnuts, but he was convinced the forest was in danger. He was a visionary and an artist and probably the right sort of person for Hungerford to tell his story to."

The three of us made the 600 m climb out of the Grose Gorge via Dockers Ladder to Perrys Lookdown together. The higher we climbed, the wetter and windier it became. Cloud swirled around us, now obscuring, now revealing the cliffs of Lockley Pylon on the far side of Govetts Gorge. Gaps in the whiteness occasionally offered glimpses down into the Grose Gorge, where Blue Gum Forest stood out by virtue of the slightly different quality of its green. Above the talus slope, the track turned into a series of steps up which, in places, we had to scramble on all fours, resting frequently to recover our breath.

The car park at Perrys Lookdown is 1570 steps from the gorge floor. Having reached it two and a half hours after setting out, we bundled ourselves into Jeff's car and raced to Blackheath for hot soup in a cosy café.

Alone among rock spires, bushwalker Richard Kerr looks from Lockley Pylon across to Fortress Hill, upper left, and the cliffs below Evans Lookout, upper right. In between is the southern arm of Govett Gorge. Walkers can descend to the gorge floor by Rodriguez Pass, which links Evans and Govetts Leap lookouts via Greaves Creek and Govetts Leap Brook. The pass, opened in 1900, was named after Thomas Rodriguez, a surveyor and Blackheath stationmaster who became a vigorous supporter of community projects. Lockley Pylon was named after John Lockley, a SYDNEY MORNING HERALD journalist who wrote about gardening and nature and helped publicise the campaign to save Blue Gum Forest.

MOUNT WILSON IS THE NAME of both a village (permanent population 30, with about 100 part-timers) and the 1000 m high mountain on which it sits, one of several basalt-capped outcrops along the Bells Line of Road. With their cool climate and rich volcanic loam, these prominences are islands of fertility in a sea of impoverished soil and once nurtured dense forests of tall eucalypts with understoreys of tree ferns and rainforest. Since Europeans arrived, however, some have been planted with exotic flora. Mount Wilson has become famous for not only its lost-world quality but also its English-style gardens.

I'd decided to visit Mount Wilson and some of the other basalt outcrops during my return trip to Sydney on Bells Line of Road after my descent into the Grose Gorge. By the end of my journey I would have completed the loop formed by the Great Western Highway (and the railway line), the Darling Causeway and Bells Line of Road and seen some of what lay within it.

The growth of the village, named after the then State Minister for Lands, John Bowie Wilson, was linked to the opening of the railway line to Lithgow in 1869. A platform named Mount Wilson was built at the site of present-day Bell in 1875, 8 km west of the Mount Wilson turn-off on Bells Line of Road.

Among the first of the wealthy to build at Mount Wilson was Richard Wynne, a businessman whose later bequest funded the Wynne Prize for landscape painting. Wynne put up a cottage in 1875 and later a large home initially named *Yarrawa* and

later *Wynstay*. George Henry Cox, grandson of the mountain roadbuilder, built *Beowang* in 1878, and Jesse Gregson, chairman of the Australian Agricultural Company, built *Yengo* in 1880, by which time eight houses were standing. Soon there was a post office, a primary school, St George's Anglican Church and a succession of stores.

Mount Wilson's residents, like home-owners in other parts of the Blue Mountains, created gardens that harked back to their beloved England. In the rich basaltic soil the imported plants exploded into growth, obscuring views of the surrounding landscape and contributing to the ambience of seclusion and isolation that still characterises the settlement. Residents lavished as much love on the village's avenues as on their gardens, lining them with Spanish chestnut, elm, plane, lime, oak, pink cherry, beech and liquidambar trees. While the gardens attract thousands of visitors in spring, some people consider the roadways to be Mount Wilson's crowning glory.

Seven out of the original eight Mount Wilson properties are famous for their gardens, as are some later ones. *Beowang*, now called *Withycombe* and owned by Helen and Gary Ghent, has 3 ha planted mainly with trees and lawn. The elegant cedar

The volcanic loam on Mount Wilson, another of the region's basalt-capped peaks, has benefited the many foreign plants that the well-to-do residents of the tiny village of the same name have propagated on its summit since the 1870s. With its cool, moist climate and rich soil, Mount Wilson is an island of fertility in a sea of impoverished terrain. In autumn the many imported trees (opposite) brush the landscape with exotic colour and carpet the lawns of the village's impressive properties with leaves. Withycombe (above left), formerly the holiday home of author Patrick White's family, is now run as an elegant guesthouse by Helen Ghent (above) and husband Gary.

Another of Mount Wilson's properties, YENGO is owned by Australian Geographic Society trustee Peter Pigott and wife Ann. Built in 1880, it has gardens designed by Charles Moore, first director of Sydney's Royal Botanic Gardens. Bronze sculptures (above) by English artists Lloyd le Blanc and Judith Holmes-Drury grace YENGO's gardens and are for sale. The Pigotts bought the property's front gate (above right) in England about 30 years ago and had local stonemasons build the pillars. An impressive remnant of Mount Wilson's original vegetation survives in the Cathedral of Ferns (opposite).

homestead, opposite the church in Church Lane, was for years the holiday home of Patrick White's family. The Nobel prize-winning author left his initials carved in a tree trunk near the side gate.

"We bought *Withycombe* in 1980 as a holiday house," Helen said. "In the mid-'80s we lived in England and found the best holidays you could have there were in bed-and-breakfasts. So when we came back here I decided to open our home to guests."

What she and Gary have created is a tasteful guesthouse that's filled with antiques, including a 1620 refectory table, and a billiard table that has been in the house since the early 1900s. For literary guests, there's also a set of Patrick White first editions. This is no ordinary bed-and-breakfast: this is dinner, bed and breakfast in refined luxury, a place that attracts an international clientele as well as Australian guests who enjoy the tranquillity of the village.

Mount Wilson offers more than just beautiful homes. It has a large picnic and camping ground set among tree ferns and tall gums on its north side, near a spectacular patch of rainforest called the Cathedral of Ferns. It also has several picturesque walks of varying difficulty and length, and – importantly for the serious outdoor adventurer – it provides access to the Wollangambe region. But beware: this is true wilderness. It may look deceptively gentle from the heights of Mount Wilson, but few tracks penetrate it and walking there requires experience and navigation skills.

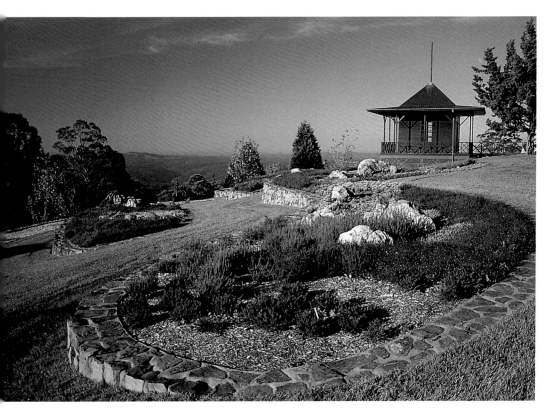

Autumn tableau (opposite) at Mount Tomah Botanic Garden.
The walls and steps (opposite, bottom right) have been built out of
some of the mountain's basalt. The 28 ha garden is one of the few
in the world where vegetation has been grouped according to its
geographical origin. It has plants from the Himalaya, western
China, South America, Africa, Europe, North America and New
Zealand, as well as Australia. Its heath and heather garden (left)
is topped by the Northern Pavilion, which offers breathtaking views
of wilderness to the north-east. The garden's South African proteas
(below) are a good source of nectar for native birds such as this
New Holland honeyeater.

On the way to the Cathedral of Ferns I had views of bush that seemed to go on
forever. I was seeing not just the Wollangambe's surroundings, in the northernmost
portion of the Blue Mountains National Park, but also a reserve that rolled for
100 km beyond it. It was Wollemi National Park, *terra incognita* to me.

As you drive back towards Sydney on Bells Line of Road, you get occasional
glimpses of the Grose Gorge's cliffs, glowing like coals, on your right before you pass
Mount Banks, another prominent basalt-capped peak. Unlike Mount Wilson, this
outcrop has been left in its natural state, and there's a good track to the top.

About 8 km further on you reach one of the biggest basalt outcrops in the Blue
Mountains region, Mount Tomah. Named Fern Tree Hill by explorer George Caley
– from the quantity of tree ferns he found growing among the coachwood, sassafras
and brown barrel on its summit – this slab of a mountain was renamed Mount Tomah
in deference to the Darug people, *tomah* reputedly being their word for tree fern.

The 1000 m high mountain has a basalt layer 100 m thick that, like other such
basalt caps, has eroded to create rich soils ideal for growing all varieties of plants.

The seasons mark their passing at Mount Tomah Botanic Garden with displays that are a visual delight (above). The garden is an educational experience all year round. One who helps enlighten the public is Rusty Worsman, Mount Tomah's educational and community programs officer (above right), seen here examining a king protea. He not only guides students and schoolchildren around the garden but also visits country schools, taking with him plant specimens to use in describing native plantlife. The garden helps in the propagation of native plants with local community Landcare groups.

French-born horticulturist Alfred Brunet and his Australian wife, Effie, who had operated a cut-flower farm on the mountain since 1934, donated their 28 ha property to Sydney's Royal Botanic Gardens in 1970. Today it specialises in cool-climate plants, in particular those of the Southern Hemisphere. Opened to the public only in 1987, it is now home to 10,000 plant species and has already gained worldwide renown. When I stopped there, I met its education and community programs officer, Adam "Rusty" Worsman.

When not guiding groups of students or schoolchildren around the gardens, Rusty, 33, can be found in the bush canyoning, walking or running. He explained that Mount Tomah was one of the few botanic gardens of the world in which plants have been divided according to their geographical origins. "This gives you an intimate feeling, like walking from room to room," he said. "And then at certain points you've got this magnificent view of the northern Blue Mountains."

Several weeks after my visit I returned to Mount Tomah to attend the official opening of the Gondwana Walk, which winds through the Gondwana Woodland beside the entrance driveway. After the opening – by Marie Moody, a presenter of the ABC program *Gardening Australia* – before about 100 people, schoolchildren from Blackheath and Bilpin public schools planted 30 young Wollemi pines.

TREE OF AGES

With its droopy, frond-like foliage, it looks like a cross between a fern and a conifer. Its bubbly bark resembles a coating of Coco Pops. It is one of the strangest – and certainly one of the rarest – trees in the world.

The Wollemi pine, which grows to 40 m, is related to the Queensland kauri, bunya, hoop and Norfolk Island pines, all members of the ancient conifer family Araucariaceae. The first of the family to be discovered, the monkey puzzle tree, was growing in the Chilean Andes region of Arauco, which gave the family its name.

The family was most common and widespread between 200 and 65 million years ago but was dying out in the Northern Hemisphere by the time the dinosaurs were vanishing. It held on in Gondwana, and survivors can be found on fragments of the former supercontinent, including South America, Australia and some Pacific islands.

Until 1994, the Wollemi pine was believed to have died out more than 100 million years ago. But in August that year, NPWS ranger David Noble and two companions abseiled into a 600 m gorge in a remote part of north-western Wollemi NP and found themselves among trees unlike any they'd seen before.

On hearing about the tree, scientists thought it must be an exotic species introduced to the park by birds. It took weeks of investigation to establish the trees' true identity. When the discovery was finally announced in December 1994, it shook the world. The tree was given the scientific name *Wollemia nobilis*, after the park and David Noble.

In May 1995, bushwalker and environmental campaigner Haydn Washington discovered a second site about a kilometre away in the same gorge. Subsequent counts established that only 38 adult trees and about 200 young ones were growing at the two sites, their location a closely guarded secret. Aerial searches have found no more stands of the pine.

Within weeks of the discoveries, the Royal Botanic Gardens was propagating the species at its Mount Annan nursery south-west of Sydney. Early in 1999, the NSW Government awarded a Queensland company a contract to cultivate Wollemi pines and sell them to the public. Profits would go towards research into the pine and other threatened species.

A Wollemi pine sapling (left) grows vigorously in Mount Tomah's Gondwana Woodland, where it was planted, along with 29 others during the opening of the Gondwana Walk in 1998. A dry Wollemi pine leaf (above) with a fossil of its 100-million-year-old ancestor. Young Wollemi pines (below) under lock and key at Mount Tomah. The pine is one of the world's rarest plants, with only 38 adult trees in the wild.

Nets (above) at BELLVUE, a fruit-growing property at Bilpin, on Bells Line of Road, protect orchards from hail. The newer nets at the top of the picture cost between $25,000 and $30,000 a hectare. Orchardist Bill Shields (right) harvests peaches on his 6 ha family farm, which produces about 120 bins (45–50 tonnes) of fruit – mainly apples with some stone fruit – in a good year. He sells all his stone fruit – such as these succulent peaches (opposite) – and 15–20 per cent of his apples at his roadside stall for five months of the year. "The farm pays for itself, though we don't make a fortune, and Julie, my wife, works as a teacher when she's not selling on the stall," Bill said.

Blue Gum Forest has been closed to camping to allow it to regenerate. Camp at Acacia Flat, 500 m up Govetts Creek from its junction with the Grose River. Fuel stoves are recommended. Remember to take all your rubbish out. There are pit toilets. For information (e.g. on fire bans, track condition) contact the NPWS headquarters at the Heritage Centre in Blackheath (see p. 41).

Mount Wilson has camping and picnicking facilities, a small shop and a tea room. Many of the private gardens are open in spring. *Withycombe* has four guest suites and offers full breakfast and dinner. Prices range from $275 per night for a single to $500 for a double, ☎ 02 4756 2177. *Wynstay* has buildings and gardens classified by the National Trust. It features a Turkish bath built in 1892, ☎ 02 9489 2230 or 02 4756 2006.

Mount Tomah Botanic Garden is open 10 a.m.–4 p.m. in winter and to 5 p.m. in summer. Entry is $5 per car or $2 per pedestrian or cyclist. The restaurant offers award-winning Australian cuisine, ☎ 02 4567 2154.

Picnickers Jan Whitford and John Culliton enjoy the winter sunshine and brisk air at Mount Wilson. The deciduous trees around them, in the village's main street, were planted by residents. Many visitors believe the settlement's avenues are as beautiful as its private gardens.

From Mount Tomah, Bells Line of Road turns west-north-west and begins to descend gradually towards the eastern escarpment of the range. By the time you reach Bilpin, a village of some 500 residents 12 km from the botanic garden, the unbroken expanse of bush has given way to orchards, many covered with vast white tents of hail netting, and emerald paddocks dotted with horses and white-painted gates. Neat farm homesteads stand off the road, and kerbside stalls tempt passing motorists with a variety of fruit, but mainly with the apples for which Bilpin is famous. At the time of my visit, the apple trees were coming into leaf and the roadside wattle was a mass of gold.

Leaving Bilpin, I continued my journey to Sydney. A glance at my map told me that the bush to the north of Bells Line of Road at this point was no longer in the Blue Mountains NP but in Wollemi, a sandstone massif crisscrossed with gorges, canyons and valleys and very few roads. I realised I'd never be able to claim I'd explored all of the Blue Mountains until I'd ventured into Wollemi, one of NSW's least accessible regions.

"A scene of great wildness"
The western edge of Wollemi

First explored in 1977 by David Noble, the NPWS project officer who found the Wollemi pine, Rocky Creek Canyon is probably one of the most popular canyons in the Blue Mountains region. Easy to walk through, it has no abseils or swims through cold pools, though you do get your feet wet. It is reached from the Glow Worm Tunnel Road.

The rain that had started during our walk in the Grose Gorge early in August persisted over the ensuing weeks. It was still pouring when we made our way into Deep Pass, on the south-western corner of Wollemi National Park, a month later.

With us were Rusty Worsman from Mount Tomah Botanic Garden and his wife Janelle. Leaving our vehicles in the car park at the top of a ridge, we trudged down the wet track to the grassy clearing of the pass. Low cloud and rain softened the hard edges of the surrounding cliffs. A group of elderly bushwalkers, looking far more cheerful than the conditions warranted, were sitting under a tarp having tea and cake.

Visitors prepared for the rough drive (not recommended for 2WD vehicles in the wet) from Bells Line of Road and the short but steep descent on foot will reap big rewards at Deep Pass. It provides camping in a serene setting and some beautiful creek destinations, with waterfalls and deep pools, within easy walking distance. For those seeking serious adventure, an awesome expanse of still mostly unexplored land spreads to the north and east. Wollemi, covering nearly 4876 sq. km, is NSW's second-largest national park after Kosciuszko and contains the State's most exten-

sive officially recognised wilderness (3610 sq. km, declared in March 1999, five months after my visit). It is the largest eucalypt-forest wilderness anywhere in the world. Although I realised I might never be lucky enough to explore more than a fraction of it in my life, it was reassuring to know it was there.

Rusty had been familiar with Deep Pass, and most of the area around it, since the age of 18. As a high-school student in the Blue Mountains village of Blaxland, he had explored Wollemi, Kanangra-Boyd and Blue Mountains national parks. And since starting work at Mount Tomah, he had been plant-collecting on the Newnes Plateau around Deep Pass.

"This is a junction, the boundary between two river catchments, the Wollangambe River on one side and the Wolgan on the other," he said. "There's plenty of water here, and the area was used by the Aborigines, probably when they were travelling through."

Almost on cue, we came across a series of hand-stencils, embellished with more recent graffiti, at the base of a cliff about 30 m high and running for 50 m. The cliff overhung at a slight angle, affording us a few metres of shelter between its

Fording the Wolgan River (right) in a 4WD presents little problem for visitors wanting to get a little closer to the ruins of the Newnes shale-oil refinery. Owners of other vehicles can park nearby and wade across the river before beginning the 1.5 km walk eastward to the historic site. Newnes, consisting of a car-camping ground and a home that was once a hotel, lies at the head of the Wolgan Valley, where the river turns east into Wollemi National Park. If, instead of heading east after crossing the river, walkers follow a track southwards, they will reach Glow Worm Tunnel. Deep Pass, off the Glow Worm Tunnel Road, is a popular bush-camping area and has dark chasms filled with tree ferns (opposite) only a short walk away. Plentiful water here ensured it was much used by Aboriginals travelling through the mountains.

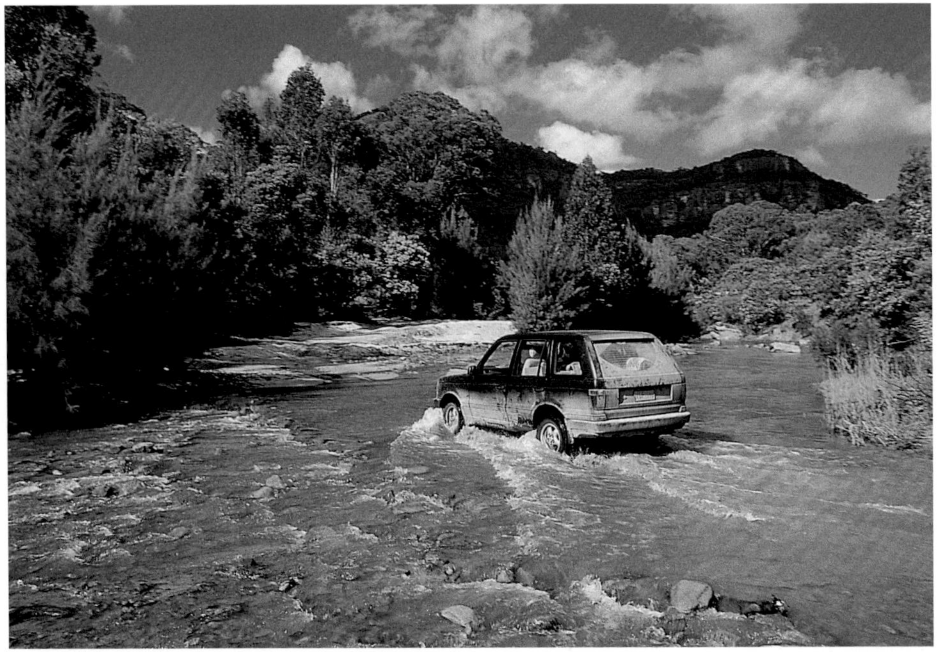

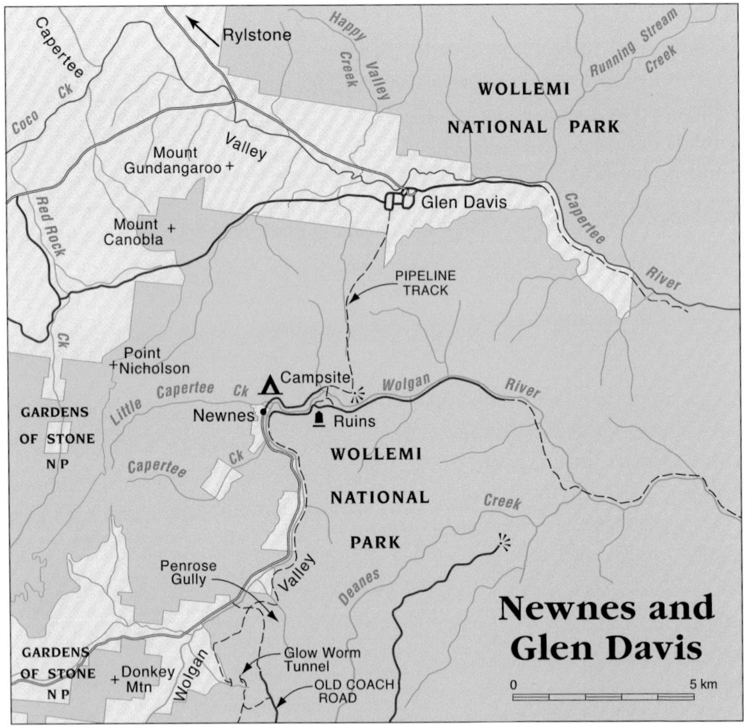

base and the dripline. Rusty pointed out small flakes of quartz, flint and jasper lying in the powdery soil under the cliff. To me they looked like ordinary pebbles, but when Rusty said "Aboriginal artefacts", I realised I was looking either at stone cutting-tools or fragments left over from their manufacture.

Leaping ahead through the wet fern and bracken, Rusty led us from one delightful waterfall to the next. It was still raining when we returned to the cars. And rain was still falling when we headed north across the Newnes Plateau on the very muddy Glow Worm Tunnel Road. About 30 km north of Lithgow, we left the Newnes State Forest and, with Wollemi NP on our right (east) and the Gardens of Stone National Park on our left, found ourselves deep in pagoda county.

Pagodas are sandstone formations that have been eroded into an infinite variety of beehive or stepped-tower shapes resembling Asian temples, some as large as buildings, some only a metre or two high. They skulked darkly among the eucalypt and wattle or stood guard in mist-shrouded ranks above gorges, the orange stripes across their grey flanks standing out like sword slashes in flesh. They gave what might have been a familiar bushscape an outlandish appearance.

The most stunning pagodas are concentrated in 53,000 ha between the Newnes Plateau and Capertee River valley. Some of the best pagoda country is found in the Gardens of Stone National Park, though many beautiful formations remain outside.

Light at the end of Glow Worm Tunnel (above) comes in shades of brilliant green, filtered by a forest of tree ferns. The glow worms that give the 400 m abandoned railway tunnel its name are the larvae of the fungus gnat, which light up their bodies to attract prey such as mosquitoes to snares made of silken threads studded with sticky droplets. Noise and light cause the worms to switch off, so visitors should be quiet and avoid using torches. Rusty Worsman (above right) explores a tumbling creek near Deep Pass.

Since pagodas are found in coal country, understandable opposition to their protection has come from coalmining companies. Conservationists, however, point to the damage caused to pagodas by mining under them and consequent subsidence. Many, having subsided by up to 1.5 m, have split, cracked or collapsed. The conflict over the issue continues.

It was still raining when we arrived at our destination, Glow Worm Tunnel, 2 km south of the Wolgan Valley. The road we'd been driving on follows the course of an abandoned railway line between Newnes Junction, on Bells Line of Road, and Newnes, a former oil-shale-mining town at the head of the Wolgan Valley. The 400 m tunnel was one of two built to ease the line's gradient from the plateau into the valley. As its name implies, nature has reclaimed the tunnel in spectacular fashion and visitors in their thousands now brave the rough road to witness the spectacle.

The four of us stumbled into the tunnel's eastern entrance, set into a cliff and clogged with ferns, 1 km beyond the parking area. Though out of the rain, we were still not free of water, since a creek runs through the tunnel. After about 50 m we were in pitch blackness. As our eyes adjusted, we began to make out pinpoints of bluish light all around us, some in clusters, some solitary. The further we tripped and blundered along the wet, boulder-strewn floor, the more lights we saw, until it seemed we were walking under a starlit sky.

Pagodas, striking sculptures created in sandstone by erosion over the past 90 million years or so, come in an infinite variety of shapes and sizes. They may stand on their own, in small clusters or in vast groups that look like ruined cities. Most are protected in the Gardens of Stone National Park, but many still lie outside it.

Bogged. The vehicle driven by Peter Meredith and Don Fuchs sinks to its axles in soft mud in Ben Bullen State Forest, just outside Gardens of Stone National Park. The incident was no reflection of the vehicle's qualities, more of those of its occupants who in the fading light found it hard to gauge the softness and depth of the black mud. It took six attempts by members of the Hartley Valley Four-Wheel Drive Club to free the vehicle. Apart from a generous covering of mud, there was no damage.

LATER THAT DAY WE LEARNT what it is to need rescuing. Not that we were in a particularly remote part of the Australian bush, just in an out-of-the-way hollow with the prospect of seeing nobody till the following weekend, when adventurous four-wheel-drivers might (or might not) come through.

Having crossed to Ben Bullen State Forest by a circuitous route, we drove due north through the headwaters of the Coxs River – literally drove *through*, since some of the creeks were flowing across the track on their way to a long swamp on our left. I reflected how, after such healthy beginnings, the river would suffer many indignities before reaching Lake Burragorang 70 km to the south-east. Drained to supply water for Wallerawang and Mount Piper power stations, it runs at less than a quarter of its natural flow rate through agricultural land south of Lithgow, picking up farm runoff, sewage and other pollutants before entering the national park system in the southern Blue Mountains.

After stopping to admire the view into the Wolgan Valley from the Great Dividing Range, we began negotiating a steep track into a small gorge, aiming to reach a camping area on Baal Bone Creek in time for a lazy evening. Rusty and Janelle, deciding the track looked too steep and muddy for their 4WD station wagon, parked and got out to walk the remaining 2 km. They were planning to return to their home in the Blue Mountains later that day, so it would be no inconvenience to walk back up to the car.

It was a wise decision. Beyond the bottom of the descent I drove our borrowed 4WD into a harmless-looking puddle. It sank to the door-sills in soft black mud. We were stuck.

Leaving Don despondently pitching a tent near our vehicle, Janelle, Rusty and I walked back to their wagon and drove to Lithgow. There I made contact with Rod Gurney, the no-nonsense president of the Hartley Valley Four-Wheel Drive Club. No worries, he said, the club would get us out.

So, like the cavalry riding to the rescue, six 4WD vehicles carrying 11 club members drove into the setting sun to Ben Bullen State Forest. I shared the cab of a ute driven by Mark Cooper, the club secretary.

It took six attempts to get us out with a snatch strap (a kind of bungee cord) attached to Rod's ute. Headlight beams pierced the deepening gloom of the gorge and engines howled. Finally, to a chorus of "Yeeha!", our vehicle was heaved from the clutches of what turned out to be a creek across the track.

Our vehicles mustered at the camping area, the remains of a farm homestead, two minutes along the track. I'd decided this was a great opportunity to discuss four-wheel-driving in national parks and wilderness declarations with members of a user group known for its strong views on these topics. Under a brilliant full moon, our collective breath rose in a cloud about our heads as the parley heated up.

The 4WD lobby's biggest bones of contention are the declaration of wilderness areas and the subsequent closure of tracks to vehicles. Under the March 1999 Wollemi wilderness declaration, the two 4WD trails across Wollemi National Park – the Hunter

Main and Wirraba trails – were due to be closed to vehicles. I could understand the four-wheel-drivers' concern that the area available to them was shrinking.

"We love the bush. We want to protect it as much as anyone else," Rod said. "Why does the Government want to lock us out?"

Rod said the umbrella body representing the 4WD groups, the Recreational Four Wheel Drive Clubs Association of NSW and the Australian Capital Territory, encouraged responsible bush driving. It had an environmental policy, ran a driver training program and planned to appoint a full-time environmental officer, he said.

"If the NPWS and the greens had their way, the frail aged and the physically handicapped would never see the bush because you need a 4WD to get out there," Mark said. "We want the Government to realise wilderness is public land that belongs to

Pantoneys Crown, the 1022 m high feature in the middle distance, dominates this vista of the Gardens of Stone National Park. Beyond lies the valley of the Capertee River. Out of the picture to the left is Baal Bone Gap, a natural pass through a range that encloses the southern sector of the park. The cliffs and pagodas here are home to banksias, dwarf she-oaks and pagoda daisies. In the eucalypt forest on the steep slopes live koalas, yellow-bellied gliders and even powerful owls.

everybody, not a select group of bushwalkers. Responsible access to wilderness areas should be afforded to all who wish to visit them."

One of the bodies supporting wilderness protection is the Colong Foundation. The organisation has always stressed that it is not people but vehicles that are excluded from wilderness. When I put Rod and Mark's views later to foundation director Keith Muir, he said his concern was that Wollemi, one of Australia's last great wild areas, would be wild no longer if more people were allowed to drive into it. "The whole area would become imbued with the character of vehicle-based activity," he said.

Keith said he saw nothing wrong with developing appropriate access and picnic facilities on the fringes of wilderness, where there was plenty to appreciate. "This would make it available to families and the average person who wants to have a bush experience but doesn't have the time for more than half a day there."

A few minutes' drive to the north of Baal Bone Gap campsite is Baal Bone Gap, a pass leading down from the Great Dividing Range into the northernmost of the three separate portions of the Gardens of Stone National Park. This portion centres on a wild mesa, called Pantoneys Crown, that rises 550 m out of a sea of ironbark and box woodland on the southern edge of the Capertee Valley. We could not resist climbing a nearby pagoda for a view to Pantoneys Crown and the landscape beyond.

I had to agree with Keith Muir that there was plenty to appreciate on the edge of Wollemi. You could spend weeks just travelling the 400 km of roads around the outside of the park and still not take it all in. And though I'm stirred by the sight of wilderness, I can also appreciate the beauty of landscapes altered by humans. The Wolgan Valley, for instance, is a uniquely picturesque blend of cultivated and wild

Like a lost city in the jungle (above), the remains of the Newnes oil-shale refinery are fast being reclaimed by nature. Established by the Commonwealth Oil Corporation and named after Sir George Newnes, the company's chairman, the refinery produced crude oil, from which were further refined petrol, kerosene, lubricating oils, fuel oil, tar and pitch between 1906 and 1923. This oven (right) is one of 120 originally built at Newnes to produce coke for steelworks and a copper smelter in Lithgow. Ninety remain, and some are in excellent condition.

terrain. And the further you drive up it, the more attractive it becomes, until you reach Newnes at the head of the valley.

Newnes was once a busy township of up to 2000 people, all of whom relied for their living on a nearby oil-shale mine and processing plant that operated, on and off, from 1906 to 1932, transporting its product to the outside world on the railway line that went through the Glow Worm Tunnel. Most of the township's dwellings were little more than wooden shacks. Today Newnes has a population of just five, and only one building survives intact – the Newnes Hotel, opened in 1907. The remains of the other structures are fast vanishing under the encroaching bush, including the most impressive ruins of them all, those of the old shale-oil plant.

The hotel stands on the opposite side of the Wolgan Road from the Wolgan River. It is an idyllic setting, with 390 m high orange sandstone crags standing guard over a lush valley. The hotel's owner since 1984, 60-year-old Stirling Butchard, reckons it's a prime location. "The view from my veranda is the best from any veranda in the nation, and that includes Sydney Harbour," he said.

So why was the hotel up for sale? When I asked Stirling this, he spilled the sorry saga of how the hotel lost its licence in 1988. After a flood damaged the building in 1986, it was taken apart and moved to higher ground. Unfortunately, because the hotel had been dismantled and rebuilt, the authorities deemed it a new structure that had to comply with current building regulations. Since it clearly did not, Stirling was forced to sell the licence and close the hotel.

Stirling said that as a result of the closure he lost $750,000 and his marriage broke up. "When the hotel was operating, it was nothing on long weekends to have 60 people in the bar and 300 out the front drinking. There'd be nine of us serving and we'd get through 14 ton of beer.

"The dreams are gone now. But one thing I haven't done is destroy the place. It's still much the same as it was."

The hotel was in disrepair but Stirling couldn't afford to renovate it. A brass finisher by trade, he was making a living mending mechanical free-sprung clocks and watches. It was time, he said, to close a chapter in his life and move on to the next, so the hotel was on the market for $500,000.

Time has taken on a new significance for Stirling Butchard (above right), proprietor of the Newnes Hotel (right). Opened in 1907, the hotel is the last of Newnes township's original buildings still standing. It lost its liquor licence in 1988 after it was dismantled and shifted to higher ground. Stirling earns a living by repairing clocks and watches. The hotel, on the market with 16 ha of land at the time of writing, is in need of extensive renovation.

A kiosk operated by Allan Watson, a historian, opens in the hotel bar at week-ends. Most of the 200 cars that come through each week are carrying visitors to the Little Capertee camping area, 1 km up the valley, from where they walk to the ruins of the shale-oil works.

The camping area is a grassy meadow of some 3 ha, so huge that the dunny looks like a tree-stump in the distance, with the Wolgan River and Little Capertee Creek flowing past on two sides. On another are great humpy cliffs of brilliant orange sandstone, craggy peaks and angry bluffs, all rising from a thick-pile carpet of dense bush. I've never seen such a spectacularly situated camping area in all my travels around Australia.

About 1.5 km down the Wolgan from the camping ground lie the ruins of the works, now managed by the NPWS. Here the Commonwealth Oil Corporation, under the chairmanship of Sir George Newnes, extracted and refined crude oil from oil-shale mined on the north side of the river. Eventually low extraction rates, high production costs and competition from cheap overseas crude killed the venture.

The main complex is on the south side and is reached, after crossing the river at the ford, along the route of the old railway, dismantled after the works closed. Don and I spent many hours exploring the ruins, starting at the beautifully built ovens in which, until 1912, coal was converted to coke for use in steelworks at Lithgow. Many of the bricks for the ovens, and the other buildings in the complex, were made on site from clay mined nearby.

The Newnes project was superseded by a processing plant at Glen Davis, 6 km to the north beyond a rough ridge. This produced petrol, gas oil, fuel oil and kerosene between 1937 and 1952 and in its heyday supported a township of 6000 people. Petrol was piped south over the ridge to Newnes and Newnes Junction. Today a walking track, the Pipeline Track, links the two derelict oil works. It's a six-hour trek for experienced walkers, beginning with a steep but picturesque climb through rainforest up a boulder-choked gully from the Wolgan River.

The Glen Davis works stand on the Capertee River, which flows east and joins the Wolgan in the centre of Wollemi to form the Colo River. None of those rivers could be called pristine. Standing on a gigantic mullock heap beside the Capertee at Glen Davis, I could just imagine the brew of pollutants that poured into the river while the plant was operating. Both the Capertee and the Wolgan flow through farmland and pick up agricultural runoff and silt before entering Wollemi. Older bushwalkers say the silt has altered the nature of the rivers in the national park, creating sandbanks and shallows and in places making walking easier than it was.

Among the first bushwalkers to traverse Wollemi were Gordon Smith and Max Gentle, both super-fit members of the Sydney Bush Walkers. In 1931 they walked from Capertee via Glen Davis and Gospers Mountain to Kurrajong in 12 days. Max described the centre of Wollemi as "a scene of great wildness rather than beauty; it could make a master bushman shudder".

An emerald meadow (opposite), surrounded by bush-clad crags and reached by crossing a shallow creek (negotiable by standard vehicles), is the site of the Newnes camping ground. A kiosk run on weekends from one of the old bars of the Newnes Hotel sells basic foods and provides information on the area. At Glen Davis, 6 km north of Newnes, the remains of a more recent oil-shale processing plant (above) stand beside the Capertee River. Glen Davis superseded Newnes and ran from 1937 to 1952. The ruins are privately owned.

A man, his horse and his dog. Farmer Allan Wales rests his mount while checking his cattle on Mount Coricudgy, where he has a grazing lease in an enclave of State forest enclosed by Wollemi National Park. Though he doesn't always see eye to eye with the NPWS, he wears their badge on his sleeve. The badge was sewn on as a joke while he was asleep and he kept it there to amaze friends and fellow farmers. About 10 km upstream of the Cudgegong River from Allan's property, KELGOOLA, lies Dunns Swamp (right), an artificial lake that has become a paradise for waterbirds. Campers are greeted every morning by scenes like this as the sun rises beyond Mount Midderula and burns the mist from the lake.

THE CONTRAST BETWEEN the eerie Glen Davis ruins and our next destination could not have been greater. Dunns Swamp, originally a chain of waterholes on the Cudgegong River, was dammed by a cement company in 1930 to create Kandos Weir. Today it is a popular car-camping area, as well as a haven for wildlife, particularly waterfowl, set among pagodas in an arm of Wollemi National Park that projects towards the small town of Rylstone.

Wiradjuri Aboriginals made their living around the waterholes for more than 20,000 years before European settlement began in 1819. They left scarred trees, stone flakes and galleries of faded hand stencils and other images.

On our first night at the swamp, I walked among the pagodas and tall angophoras under a rising full moon so bright I had to shade my eyes when facing it. The tree trunks glowed dully, the pagodas reclining like enormous prehistoric creatures among them. I climbed the biggest pagoda I could find, careful not to trample the heath growing in the small depressions. Life was precarious enough for these plants without having humans' boots making it harder. The higher I climbed, the louder became a sound that at first I took to be the muttering of many people. A chill ran down my spine. I had the irrational notion that I was about to walk into a Wiradjuri *wagaji*, or dance. When I topped the pagoda's summit, the lake spread below me like mercury beyond a fringe of trees. At the same time the voices became the calls of thousands of frogs.

At dawn next morning the frogs were still calling among the lakeside sedges and grasses when I crawled out of my tent and set off along the lakeside. A blanket of thin mist covered the water, softening the hard edges of the rock that spilled from the fringing bush to the shore here and there.

I found Don at Pagoda Lookout, on the summit of a pagoda at the western end of the swamp. On the eastern horizon, my eye was drawn to a flat-topped mountain that wore a toupee of smooth cloud. It was Mount Coricudgy, in Coricudgy State Forest, at 1256 m the highest of the Greater Blue Mountains region's basalt-capped outcrops but by no means the most extensive.

Keen to discover what lay under the cloud, we drove to the mountain's summit later that morning. The vegetation changed abruptly from eucalypt woodland to rainforest as we climbed the muddy track, and in no time we were among tree ferns and sassafras, though the understorey was noticeably grazed. About halfway up we passed the turn-off of the Hunter Main Trail, a popular 4WD route across to the eastern edge of Wollemi (closed five months later by the March 1999 wilderness declaration).

Beyond a boggy patch on the flat summit, we were driving on a track of familiar black basalt soil when ahead of us we spotted a horseman accompanied by a cattle dog. They were about to veer off through the trees when we caught up with them.

The rider was an austere-looking man with long, grey sideboards, heavy eyelids and a determined jaw. He sat erect on his chestnut horse, a battered hat on his head

High on a pagoda near Dunns Swamp, environmentalist Haydn Washington (right) finds a sample of the barbed-wire bush (below), a native pea that was placed on the endangered list as a result of his work. The plant is a member of the Pultenaea group, which comprises about 100 species. "At least a quarter of the plants here grow only on pagodas," Haydn said. "Those that fail to compete elsewhere can normally find a niche among pagodas because there are so many microclimates and they are protected from fire. They are like defeated races of people who have fled to the mountains." Unfortunately, many plant species are slipping into extinction without us realising, according to Haydn. One of his aims is to publicise the plight of plants around Rylstone. "We're trying to get people to realise they're living in an amazing place."

and stockwhip coiled around his neck. He was Allan Wales, cattle farmer of *Kelgoola*, a 2262 ha property in the valley we'd driven through to reach the mountain.

We yarned, he on his horse, we in our high-tech machine. Our conversation covered the kinds of issues that arouse the passions of most farmers hereabouts – wilderness declarations, the perceived reluctance of the NPWS to burn off, and the like. Allan's concern was that Mount Coricudgy – on which he has grazing rights – might be incorporated in the national park and officially declared wilderness.

"When we bought the property the grazing lease on this mountain was part of the deal," he said. "If it becomes national park I don't know what I'll do. I'm 67 and I don't feel like starting again. I'll probably retire and sell out."

He added after a moment: "No, maybe I'll stop here and just annoy the bastards!"

(In the event, under the March 1999 wilderness declaration, less than 7 per cent of 7300 ha Coricudgy State Forest was to be added to the national park.)

Two hours later I was talking to a man with concerns very different from Allan's, though his hat was just as battered. Haydn Washington is a tall, well-built man who arrived at our rendezvous in a minuscule 4WD vehicle. Don and I followed him into Currant Mountain Gap, inside the national park and a couple of kilometres southwest of Dunns Swamp, to see a species of flower – *Pultenaea* "Olinda", a native pea sometimes called the barbed-wire bush – which he had found in the area and which had recently been placed on the endangered list as a result of his nominating it.

Haydn, 44, works as an environmental consultant. He's a councillor on the Australian Conservation Foundation and president of the Rylstone District Environment Society, which he founded after settling in the area five years ago. During the 1970s, as secretary of the Colo Committee, he was a leading light in the campaign that resulted in the Colo wilderness being dedicated as Wollemi National Park in 1979. The Colo Committee and the Colong Committee subsequently went on to campaign successfully to have the Gardens of Stone National Park created.

His environmental work was founded on solid experience of the bush. At 18 he walked 120 km down the Colo River. In 1995, he discovered the second stand of Wollemi pines. "Having bushwalked in Wollemi for 23 years, I had some idea where to look," he said.

Near the summit of a pagoda we found what we were looking for. It was a barbed-wire bush, with bunches of golden blooms, in a spot where Haydn had not documented it before. A little further on we found another, and then another. By the end of our exploration we'd counted 13.

The following day Don and I drove north to 1150 m high Nullo Mountain, the most extensive basalt outcrop in the northern Blue Mountains area. Surrounded by Wollemi NP, it is about 22 km long by 14 km at its widest. Much of it is covered by Nullo Mountain State Forest and the rest by farms. Settlers began to occupy the mountain in the 1840s and soon were driving stock to graze in the Widden Valley, 20 km to the north-east as the crow flies. Heading out along the Myrtle Gully Trail, we followed in their footsteps.

The track re-entered national park for a while, then crossed well-grassed paddocks shared by livestock and swamp wallabies. At *Box Ridges*, cattle farmer Russell Cooper unlocked a gate to let us continue into Wollemi National Park. Basalt and sandstone soils alternated in a geological roller-coaster as we drove into ever more rugged country, with occasional glimpses to the north of pagoda-like outcrops crowning thickly forested ridges. From one hairpin bend we had an impressive view of Wedding Cake Mountain and the Yodeller Range.

Finally we began to descend steeply into dense rainforest on Myrtle Creek. After crossing and recrossing the creek a number of times, we emerged onto the soft paddocks of *Myrtle Grove*, a cattle property run by Bill and Joan Tindale and one of the many fingers of farmland that poke into Wollemi's brain-shaped northern extremity. Bill's family had been farming in the Widden Valley since 1836, and though his father, Noel, had died only two weeks previously, the couple greeted us with all the warmth we had come to expect from people living in remote parts of the region.

We'd reached the limit of the Greater Blue Mountains area. Although we hadn't seen much of Wollemi's centre, we intended to remedy that on the last part of our journey, the return to Sydney along the national park's eastern flank.

TRAVEL ADVICE

Deep Pass offers excellent family camping in beautiful surroundings, but anyone intending to cover distance on foot from there should be experienced at bushwalking and navigating, and carry suitable provisions and gear.

Glow Worm Tunnel can be reached on foot from several points, depending on how far you feel like walking. The longest walk, about 8 km return (or 4 hours), is from the Wolgan Valley Road, where you must park on the western side of the Old Ford.

At Newnes, the main car-camping area (with pit toilets) is the Little Capertee site. A smaller site lies on the other side of the Wolgan River. The river crossing is straightforward in a 4WD. The Newnes Kiosk is open at weekends, ☎ 02 6355 7355, <http:/lisp.com.au/~newnesk>. More information from NPWS headquarters at the Heritage Centre in Blackheath (see p. 41).

Glen Davis shale-oil plant ruins are privately owned. Enquire at the Glen Davis Guest House about visits, ☎ 02 6379 7271.

Dunns Swamp has an attractive, low-key car-camping area among pagodas beside the lake. There are pit toilets. A number of tracks lead around the lake to lookouts and picnic sites. Swimming and canoeing are popular. More information from the NPWS Mudgee office, ☎ 02 6372 3122.

If intending to drive on the Myrtle Gully Trail, note that there are locked gates at *Box Ridges*, ☎ 02 6379 6222 (at least the night before arriving) and *Myrtle Grove*, ☎ 02 6547 0503 (at least 24 hours before).

It's all glow. Rusty and Janelle Worsman prepare to enter Glow Worm Tunnel, which once echoed to the chuff and hiss of steam locomotives travelling between Newnes and Bells Line of Road.

The middle of nowhere

Wollemi's north and east

Beneath a ragged spur in the 250 m deep Colo Gorge, bushwalkers Don and Ben Folbigg cross the Colo River at its junction with Canoe Creek, in the south-east sector of Wollemi National Park. The Colo, created by the union of the Capertee and Wolgan rivers, exits the park at Colo village, some 30 km south-east of here as the crow flies.

A wedge-tailed eagle flapped heavily across the track 30 m ahead. In its talons it carried an animal with a long bushy tail that swung freely with each flap of the great wings. Three of us in the car meant three different views on what the prey was. Yodelling angrily, a magpie chased the wedgie off through the trees.

The little drama made my day. We'd re-entered northern Wollemi through a property named *The Ranch*, at the head of the Martindale Creek valley. From there we'd negotiated an incredibly steep and rutted track to the top of a ridge and driven through the *Cowparlour*, a private grazing lease. Just after one of several creek crossings, we'd stopped to let a mature red-bellied black snake slither lazily off the track. Turning west at Raspberry Junction, we'd seen a mass of birdlife – eastern rosellas, king parrots, sulphur-crested cockatoos, black-faced cuckoo-shrikes. And then the eagle.

My son Nick had joined us for the last leg of our trip. He quickly entered into the spirit of our venture, pointing out different bird species and the numerous rock orchids that grew beside the track. Fire had recently raged through this part of the park, but the bush was regenerating rapidly, with young red leaves sprouting from the

trunks of eucalypts. Grass trees, those consummate survivors, were flowering, their blackened spears covered in a fuzz of tiny creamy-white blooms.

At Raspberry Junction we'd joined the Hunter Main Trail. I knew that if we went far enough along it we'd reach Three Ways junction, where the trail turned west towards Mount Coricudgy. We decided to turn around and make for Kings Cross, where we would turn north-east up the Commission Road.

We stopped for lunch at the end of a detour about 1 km short of 522 m high Sheepskin Mountain. The detour led to two corrugated iron buildings collectively named Sheepskin Hut. One was a stall built on piles and the other a hut with a fireplace, two small windows, a metal table-cum-shelf built into one wall and a dirt floor. These relics of mid-19th-century attempts to run sheep in the area stand in the catchment of Doyles Creek.

One of the first Europeans to penetrate this area was William Parr, a mineralogist, who with four others set out from Windsor in 1817 to try to find an overland route to the Hunter River. Trekking by way of Putty Creek, the MacDonald River and Howes Valley Creek, the party reached

Normally spear-straight, the flowering spike (above) of this grasstree in northern Wollemi National Park has grown into a snake shape. Grasstrees, related to lilies and uniquely Australian, are among the first plants to regenerate after bushfires. The Wollemi floral gallery opposite comprises, clockwise from top left: a patersonia or native iris, whose showy flowers last only a few hours; a rock orchid, which favours sunny spots on sandstone outcrops and cliffs; a wax flower, a small woody shrub that thrives in Wollemi's sandy soils; and a common sundew, which traps insects in its sticky hairs.

a valley, probably that of Doyles Creek, from which they could see what Parr described as a "fine open part of land … which had every appearance of a river running through it". However, instead of pushing on to the Hunter, Parr turned south-west to try to reach Bathurst. Bushfires, probably lit by Aboriginals to drive them away, forced the party to abandon the attempt and return south-eastwards.

In 1819 an expedition led by John Howe, a farmer and chief constable of Windsor, reached Doyles Creek in 13 days. On two subsequent expeditions, Howe found easier access to the Hunter via Darkey Creek and the site of present-day Bulga. This route is followed by today's Putty Road.

A visitors' book at Sheepskin Hut, provided by the NPWS, had entries going back to 7 September 1991. Some complained of rubbish (though I found the place clean). A few, by a twist of logic, blamed the NPWS for this, though others praised the service for looking after the relics so well.

That afternoon we set up camp on a hill north-east of Kings Cross that gave us a view across the entire expanse of northern Wollemi, past Mount Monundilla to Mount Coricudgy, 50 km away. All I could see was wave after wave of bush rolling to the horizon, with here and there a prominence, a basalt peak.

Next morning, as though to underline the vulnerability of this landscape, I had an altogether different view. We were driving north along the Commission Road, accompanied by high-tension power lines that had joined us at Kings Cross, when, topping a rise, we saw where they were leading. On the flats of the Hunter Valley nearly 30 km away, the cooling towers of two coal-fired power stations (Liddell and Bayswater) poured steam into a band of low raincloud. All around them lay open-cut coalmines, artificial lakes and railway lines. It was a world I'd almost forgotten.

We left the park soon afterwards at Appletree Flat and, in increasingly heavy rain, drove around its north-eastern bulge to the village of Bulga and then to *Glen Ann*, a 320 ha dairy farm on Bulga Creek, just off the Putty Road. In a cliff-line above the track that leads to the homestead is an overhang about 15 m long by 5 m high. On climbing to it, we found not only that it was deep and dry but also that it had a commanding view over the Bulga Creek valley to Yengo National Park. For the artists who drew the powerful ochre figure on its rear wall, this would have been important.

The figure's outstretched arms were twice as long as normal on a human body. White circular eyes occupied most of the head, and a lozenge-shaped patch of white covered the lower abdomen. White lines ran from the upper arms towards the legs. Under the arms were stencils of hands, boomerangs and what looked like spears and other tools. The painting was first documented in 1893 by Robert Mathews, an ethnologist and surveyor.

With us at the site were Glen Morris, NPWS Aboriginal sites officer; Victor Perry, cultural manager for the Wonarua Tribal Council; and Noelene Smith, who, with husband Rodney, runs *Glen Ann*.

The sensual shapes and soft colours in a sandstone overhang (this page) beside the Hunter Main Trail in northern Wollemi delight the artistic eye. Created by wind, moisture and temperature change over thousands of years, such shapes often provide shelter for a variety of creatures. Nearby, native wasps had covered the overhang's ceiling with a small city of nests. The tawny frogmouth (opposite) spends the daytime hours sitting stock-still in a tree, often pressed against the trunk or a branch and so well camouflaged that even close up it is hard to make out against the bark. At night it perches watchfully on branches or fence posts. On spying an insect or small animal, it glides silently down and pounces like a kookaburra.

Glen, one of the Dhungutti people from further north, has lived in the Hunter district for 17 years. Softly spoken and articulate, he told us the figure was that of Baiame, an all-embracing spirit-being. After creating all things on earth, Baiame journeyed among his people imparting knowledge of law and ceremony. Then he returned to the sky to watch over his creation, stepping off nearby Mount Yengo and in the process flattening its summit.

"Baiame is depicted here as the keeper of this valley, looking out over it and embracing it. This story is told by Victor's people, the Wonarua, though the belief in Baiame extends from Queensland to the south coast of NSW," Glen said.

"The white dot on Baiame is the centre of his being, where his power comes from. The big white eyes emphasise his all-seeing power. The four lines coming down from each arm identify him as a deity."

European colonisation dealt a swift and devastating blow to thousands of years of indigenous culture. These two portraits of NSW Aboriginals were made by Frenchman Nicolas Martin Petit, artist with explorer Thomas Nicolas Baudin's scientific expedition around Australia in 1800–03. They are among a limited collection of art that shows Australia's indigenous people before European culture swamped theirs. Victor Perry (opposite), left, and Glen Morris examine the painting of creator spirit-being Baiame in an overhang on GLEN ANN, *a dairy farm on the edge of the north-eastern sector of Wollemi National Park. Although the age of the painting is unknown, people are believed to have been visiting the cave for more than 4000 years.*

BAIAME

A belief in Baiame, his name varying slightly with language or dialect, is widespread in eastern Australia. In NSW, his influence is absent only from the north-west corner.

Creator-hero and lawmaker, Baiame also features in many stories told to children. Related to the south-east wind and the native bees, he brings rain and plenty to the land.

Glen said that although it was not clear how long the figure had been on the wall, deposits excavated from the floor of the shelter had been radiocarbon dated to 5000–4000 years. "But the people would probably have been coming here a lot longer," he added. Most rock art in the Greater Blue Mountains area goes back that far, but there was a period of more intensive artistic production between 3000 and 1000 years ago.

At the time the Europeans arrived, the Wonarua occupied the middle Hunter region around northern Wollemi. To the south, around present-day Putty and Mellong Swamp, lived the Darkinjang, whose territory bordered that of the Darug, in the Hawkesbury-Nepean district. The Darug's southern neighbours were the Gundungurra. Undoubtedly these tribes would have crossed Wollemi, possibly to wage war on, but more likely to trade with, the Wiradjuri on the western side.

The impact of European colonisation on Aboriginal society was catastrophic. The original inhabitants were not only killed by the colonists and their diseases but to a lesser extent by fellow Aboriginals when, driven from their own ancestral lands, they encroached on those of other groups. By the 1840s the survivors were drifting into towns to live on the fringes of white society.

The Wonarua suffered as much as any. Today little of their ancient knowledge remains and for people like Glen and Victor, whose job is to piece it together, record it and ensure its survival, the task is particularly difficult. One direct effect of this is that the regular and essential retouching of art, such as this image of Baiame, becomes impossible because there is nobody left who knows what it should look like.

During the Dreaming, Baiame travelled about the country, sometimes accompanied by his wives, sons and a brother, setting in place the laws governing the earth and everything on it. His keeping places – often set aside as water reserves or sanctuaries for certain plants, animals or, in some cases, insects – are marked by carved trees, paintings and engravings, stone arrangements or soil sculptures.

"Because we don't have the elders with the knowledge any more, we'd probably have to go by the information recorded by Mathews when retouching this," Victor said.

From *Glen Ann*, we drove south along the Putty Road, through the steep valley of Darkey Creek, where rainforest merged with eucalypt woodland, past occasional farm clearings, with paddocks, modest homesteads and collections of derelict tractors and trucks. Although Yengo NP would accompany us on our left (the east) consistently to the end of our journey, Wollemi NP on the right gave way temporarily to State forest and farmland after 10 km. We were moving out of Wonarua lands into those of the Darkinjang.

We arrived at Putty, a village with a handful of houses and a hall 3 km off the Putty Road, in time for the Putty Spring Fair. Stalls were doing good business in a paddock behind the hall, and displays, competitions and other events were taking place in front of the hall and in a neighbouring paddock.

One display caught my attention. A man in a small enclosure was handing out Australian native reptiles for a wide-eyed audience of adults and children to handle. While a diamond python, a shingleback and a bluetongue were doing the rounds, the man placed a lace monitor (goanna) across his shoulders and delivered a carefully composed talk describing the creatures and emphasising the need for people, particularly rural people, to care for Australian wildlife.

Transport old and new (opposite). A bullock team makes an eye-catching contrast with more modern forms of transport on the main street in Putty, a tiny settlement off the Putty Road, during the local spring fair. Warily eyeing the team are Sue Meredith, daughter Georgina, 5, and author Peter Meredith. Children enjoyed the fair as much as their parents. A sack race (above left) gets off to a flying start outside the village hall, and 6-year-old Jared Meeres-Wilson (above), of Putty, meets a live version of the creature painted on his face. The snake, a diamond python, is being held by its handler, wildlife educator Anthony Stimson, who was putting on a display at the fair.

GOING, GONE

About 40 of the Greater Blue Mountains region's 400 animal species are rare or threatened. According to the NPWS World Heritage nomination document, most of these are birds or mammals, though there are a handful of reptiles.

Six animal species that were recorded in the past have not been seen lately. Another five are known to have become extinct in the area, including three kinds of bettong and the eastern quoll.

The area has 14 vulnerable or threatened animals, including the spotted-tailed quoll, the koala, the yellow-bellied and squirrel gliders, the long-nosed potoroo and the brush-tailed rock wallaby. Seven of the endangered animals are bats; nine bird species are rare or threatened; and four reptile species are endangered.

The broad-headed snake, listed as threatened, is generally found only in the east of the region. The western Blue Mountains water skink is a rare species found only in the region at Wentworth Falls, Leura and the Newnes Plateau. The green and golden bell frog, which is listed as threatened, has been recorded only in the upper Colo River.

Though dangerous, some of the region's snake species are themselves in danger. The broad-headed snake (opposite left) is listed as vulnerable and is restricted to a 250 km radius of Sydney. The tiger snake (opposite above) is named for the yellow bands that sometimes adorn its body. Growing to 1.2 m, it hunts mostly by day and is fond of frogs. The common death adder (opposite below) often lies in leaf litter, where it is beautifully camouflaged. When aroused, it strikes rapidly and repeatedly.

At 12 cm in length, the common green tree frog is among Australia's largest frogs. One of 34 frog species found in the Blue Mountains region, it is usually bright green but is sometimes brown or even blue. Its scientific name, LITORIA CAERULEA, is misleading: "caerulea" means "blue", and derives from a bottled specimen that had lost its yellow pigment and thus appeared blue. Many country people like to have green tree frogs around the house because they are enthusiastic insect eaters.

MITCH REARDON

Previously shot and poisoned because of the havoc it wreaked on domestic poultry, the spotted-tailed quoll (above) is now listed as vulnerable in the Blue Mountains region and across NSW. A graceful and agile climber, it is a nocturnal hunter that preys on birds, mammals, reptiles and insects. Bushwalkers trekking through the Blue Mountains woodlands may come across a lace monitor (above right) clinging to a tree trunk and trying to achieve invisibility. Growing to 2 m or more, this goanna species is common in the region. The female lays her eggs in termite mounds, where constant warmth incubates them. As its name implies, the eastern water dragon (right) prefers a watery environment, where it hunts frogs and other small aquatic creatures.

The reptile man was 30-year-old Anthony Stimson. After he'd dislodged the reluctant goanna from his back – by persuading it to climb on his hat and then removing the hat – he told me he had combined scientific and educational qualifications and experience into a career as a freelance wildlife educator. Working with a collection of animals that were either orphaned, injured or came from private collections, he puts on displays and presentations at schools, parties, fairs and other events. He invariably uses the animals as vehicles for a conservation message.

"I usually carry about half a dozen with me for my demonstrations; maybe a possum, a tawny frogmouth, a kookaburra, a diamond python or two and a green tree frog," he said.

"I use the frogmouth to talk about the adaptations that animals have for surviving in the bush and also about how pesticides and introduced animals like foxes are killing so many off."

Anthony's passion is reptiles, as I learnt when I visited him at his home at Colo Heights, 55 km to the south on the Putty Road. There he and his wife Kim share a 16 ha bush block on the edge of Wollemi with 100 animals representing 40 species, nearly all of which can be found in the Greater Blue Mountains area. "Wollemi is a vital habitat for a huge range of creatures," Anthony said.

Licensed by Agriculture NSW to exhibit native animals, Anthony used to work as an education officer and keeper at Featherdale Wildlife Park, in Sydney's west, until 1997. These days, as well as running his displays, he's occasionally called in to assess koala habitat when Hawkesbury City Council is considering development applications.

Anthony's reptiles are housed in temperature-controlled conditions in an extension of his home. He showed us a pair of young diamond pythons that moved in unison as they inspected his face. Then he brought out an adult female diamond python and a number of venomous snakes, including a tiger snake, a red-bellied black, an eastern brown and a broad-headed snake (listed as threatened in the Greater Blue Mountains area).

As always, Anthony had a conservation message to impart, in this case about an activity that makes his blood boil – the theft of rock from the bush. Despite greater vigilance by the NPWS, people still drive trucks and vans into the national park and load them up with rock, which eventually ends up in gardens across the city.

"Bush-rock gathering has greatly affected snakes, because they like to shelter under rocks and ledges," Anthony said. "In my view it's a cancer that's destroying habitat and devastating Wollemi."

Bush-rock gathering is just one of the illicit activities the NPWS has to deal with in the Greater Blue Mountains national parks. At Mellong Swamp, about 20 km south of the Putty turnoff on the Putty Road, Don, Nick and I rendezvoused with NPWS field officer Anthony Johnson, 30. There, beside Kings Waterhole, a small, reed-fringed lagoon beneath a conical hillock only a few minutes from the road, Anthony reeled off a list that amazed me.

The possum that Anthony Stimson is handling was blinded by a cat. She is one of the 100 animals he has in his collection, many of which he uses in his educational displays and lectures. "When I show her, kids immediately respond with sympathy and it drives home the message about keeping your cats indoors at night," Anthony said. "A single cat can kill 1000 or more animals a year. If one kid learns to keep his or her cat in at night it's an achievement."

Morning mist (opposite) clears from the bluffs above Canoe Creek, which joins the Colo River in the Colo Gorge a few hundred metres from here. The creek's name is something of a misnomer: the watercourse is so narrow and boulder-choked that no craft other than a toy one could float in it. It flows through a dense rainforest of turpentine, lilly pilly and tree-fern. Rotting logs (below) lie across it in many places, balancing on moss-cloaked rocks and making progress difficult.

It included riding unregistered trail bikes, pig-dogging, dumping stolen vehicles – and rubbish by the truckload – illegal four-wheel-driving, littering, shooting and trapping wildlife, marijuana growing and rave parties. All this on top of what were now beginning to look to me like run-of-the-mill problems – the introduced animals and plants. I marvelled at the commitment of people who continued to work for the welfare of the bush in the face of such obstacles.

I looked about. I knew that beyond the waterhole the swamp straddled Mellong Creek, which eventually joined Wollemi Creek deep inside the national park. Wollemi Creek in turn joined the Colo River further to the south. Around the waterhole, dense tussocky grass covered the floor of a sparse but attractive woodland of bloodwood, grey gum and scribbly gum, with an understorey of wattle that was now in flower. Everywhere I looked I could see greenhood orchids, quivering in the rain. It was a soothing scene through which I could imagine Darkinjang people striding confidently about their business.

Anthony, a tough, wiry bloke with a strong-featured face, said that, despite the activities he'd just mentioned, Mellong Swamp remained a delightful spot and many of the people who came here were campers "with a much more sustainable outlook on life". Education was gradually changing attitudes towards the bush, he said. "It filters up from the kids. The kids are good but often their parents have old, ingrained habits."

CONFRONTED BY ALL THE ACTIVITIES that Anthony had described, it would be hard to disagree with the view of Colong Foundation director Keith Muir about the impact of roads on wild places. I pondered this as we made our way along Grassy Hill Track, which leaves the Putty Road about 20 km south of Mellong Swamp. After about 10 km, we parked at a locked gate, and continued along the closed track on foot. Our destination was a bend in the Colo River at its junction with Canoe Creek below Alidade Hill.

The 30-minute walk brought us to the start of a walking track leading off to the left. Just before it began to drop sharply, we detoured to the west for a view of our destination. Pushing through a dense scrub of flowering native holly, we found a cliff giving us a clear view 200 m down into the Colo Gorge. My diary records my impressions:

"A staggering sight. Far below us, the golden river, with its white sands, did a U-bend around a huge outcropping spur. The sound of rapids reached us, a continuous mild thunder. It was such wild and beautiful country, harsh, rugged, rough but incredibly beautiful, with soft edges of sand and gentle vegetation … Such an untamed scene only two and a half hours from Sydney. Amazing!"

I was about to make some remark about there being no sign of humanity when Don said: "Look, campers down there on the big sand dune."

As we began the climb down to Canoe Creek, I thought of Neville Wran, NSW Premier from 1976 to 1986, who made this descent in November 1979 with members of the Colong and Colo committees.

"I was told it was a stroll of three miles down a creek. I now realise that some features of the trip had not been brought to my attention," Wran joked later. "That was a cruel climb."

Haydn Washington, Colo Committee secretary, was Wran's personal guide on the walk. Taking politicians into the bush was a tactic environmentalists had used successfully in the past to persuade them to create national parks. In fact, in April 1979 the State Government had already announced it was going to declare the Northern Division of Myles Dunphy's Blue Mountains National Park proposal. Wollemi NP came into being on 14 December 1979. Most of the area covered by Myles's 1932 proposal was now officially protected, although there would be some significant additions later.

The creation of Wollemi NP came after a spirited campaign led by the Colo Committee and supported by the Colong Committee and a handful of other groups. They had been spurred into action by several plans to develop the Colo area.

Development had been on the cards for more than a century. The Colo had been eyed in the 1870s as a route for a railway line to the west, and in the late 1890s there had been plans for a hydro-electric scheme on the river. In the early 1970s the NSW Electricity Commission was considering building a giant coal-fired power station on the Newnes Plateau and damming the Colo to supply its cooling water. AUSTRALIAN GEOGRAPHIC founder Dick Smith became involved in the campaign in May 1978 when he paid for a full-page advertisement in *The Sydney Morning Herald* saying: "Colo River – NSW Lake Pedder?"

THE PARKS PEOPLE VISIT

More than 2.3 million people visited the national parks and reserves of the Greater Blue Mountains area in 1997, the latest year for which figures are available. Most went to the Blue Mountains National Park and Jenolan Caves. The NPWS's estimates are as follows:

Blue Mountains NP	1,935,000
Jenolan Caves reserve	270,000
Wollemi NP	80,000
Kanangra-Boyd NP	40,000
Gardens of Stone NP	5000
Nattai NP	1000
TOTAL	2,331,000

The combination of beauty and harshness (opposite) has long attracted self-reliant wilderness-lovers to Colo Gorge and the surrounding country. Though he never explored the area himself, Myles Dunphy included it in his 1932 Greater Blue Mountains National Park proposal. The 80 km long gorge is said to be the longest such gorge in NSW.

South-west of Colo Heights, the Colo River emerges from Wollemi National Park into agricultural land. The poplar plantation (above) was part of a failed matchwood venture. Bob Turners Track, less than 2 km to the north, offers great views and access to swimming spots. Further downstream there are sites for family camping, picnicking, canoeing and swimming.

In addition, various plans had been put forward for improved tourist facilities, including roads, lookouts and a bridge (supposedly bigger than Sydney Harbour Bridge) over the Colo Gorge. When the national park was declared, it was named after a creek rather than the area's major river for political reasons – the Government felt the name Colo would have linked the park too closely with the Colo Committee and its campaign.

I could understand how an unfit politician might find the descent a bit of a struggle. Scrambling down the rocky track, we dropped quickly from eucalypt woodland into dark rainforest. On reaching Canoe Creek, we walked down its boulder-strewn course under huge turpentines and lilly pillies, past tree ferns and vine thickets, over fallen tree trunks rotting damply under carpets of moss. Then, taking us by surprise, the blindingly white sand dune we'd seen from the cliff rose before us. Beyond a thicket of river oaks we found one of the campers sitting in the shade.

He was 49-year-old Don Folbigg, a Newcastle carpenter. He was tanned and fit-looking, with a well-trimmed grey beard. Later, when we explored the river together, I discovered just how fit he was. He told us he and his 20-year-old son, Ben, had been camped at the spot for a couple of nights. Ben had gone down the river to fish.

As we snacked and yarned, I was unable to keep my eyes off the sight before us. Directly opposite, the spur that forces the river to bend rose like a rusting, battle-scarred warship, full of holes and rents and covered in a scaffolding of scraggly trees. The river, its water the colour of weak tea, rode around it on rippled sand, a crescent-shaped sandbank slicing it into two streams. I could see along both arms of the U-bend, two almost identical gorges heading west. The scene was so surreal I felt I was looking at it on a giant movie screen. It took me a long while to appreciate that, if I wanted to, I could walk into it.

I did. Wading, sometimes sinking to my thighs in quicksand, diving into deep pools, floating on my back and looking up at cliffs that seemed to have been created by a crazy extrusion machine, following tortoise tracks on white beaches, chasing smelt fingerlings in shallow pools, sunning myself dry.

We were joined by Ben, an environmental science student at Newcastle University. He had a skinhead haircut and frame so slight that I felt he'd struggle with an empty daypack, let alone a full bushwalking rucksack. Yet he talked of marathon walks he'd done and of plans for a 30-day walk in the near future. Here was a "hard trailer" who would have stirred Myles Dunphy's heart. He proved the point when we climbed out of the gorge, leading all the way and carrying a heavier load than the rest of us combined.

Before we parted company, I asked the father-and-son duo what had attracted them to Wollemi.

Ben replied: "It's fantastic that you can be in the middle of nowhere and yet be so close to the city."

EPILOGUE

From Alidade Hill, the Colo meanders southward to its junction with the Wollangambe River. There it turns east and, after three last great bends, it emerges near Upper Colo into a world shaped by human hand.

At Alidade Hill, as on all the tracks that pierce Wollemi's margin, you have a choice. You can either plunge from the end of the track into the web of sandstone gorges, and if you're a strong bushwalker, a good navigator and have come well equipped, you'll emerge safe and satisfied days later. Or you can return to the east, as we did, to the Putty Road and continue your journey in a comfortable car.

At Colo Heights we turned south, driving with Wollemi NP on our right and farmland on our left. At a locality named Ward Park we met the Colo River again. Here the parked cars of swimmers and boaters lined the road and the banks looked well trodden. We followed the Colo towards the village of Colo through a valley of grazing paddocks made lush by the recent rain. Apart from the eucalypt scrub on the surrounding sandstone hills, it looked, Don said, just like his native Bavaria. At Colo, the riverside flats were awash with daytrippers picnicking, barbecuing, swimming and canoeing. The nearby petrol station was selling more fast food than petrol.

We retraced our route to Ward Park, turned south and re-entered the national park beyond Upper Colo. At an attractive car-camping area on Wheeny Creek, splashing children scattered from the causeway at our approach. It being late on Sunday, most of the campers had returned to the city. We found Anthony Johnson there keeping an eye on things.

Continuing south, we climbed to the top of a bushy ridge, past a recently burnt-out car and on towards Blaxlands Ridge. Before we knew it, the bush gave way to emerald paddocks with trim homes and well-fed horses. On the eastern skyline we could see Sydney's Centrepoint Tower, yet only an hour ago we'd been in a place where you might not meet other people for weeks. I laughed aloud at my good fortune to be living in a city that had one of the world's wildest places in its backyard.

A young diamond python (opposite) graces a waratah above the Colo River. Plants as much as animals characterise the area's uniqueness. The higher parts of the Colo Gorge's sides are clad in stringybark, ironbark, blue gum, wattle and bloodwood. Lower down grow figs, turpentine and casuarina. Beside the river, water gums and clusters of ferns take the hard edges off the boulders. The river is home to eels, perch, gudgeon, smelt and frogs. A veteran walker reported recently that the character of the river has been changed since the 1930s by the deposition of silt carried from the farmland in the Wolgan and Capertee valleys.

TRAVEL ADVICE

Since this book was researched and written, the NSW Government has declared 75 per cent of Wollemi NP under the 1987 Wilderness Act. As a result, both the Wirraba and Hunter Main trails remain open only to visitors on foot or mountain bike. The far north-western, north-eastern, south-eastern and some western sectors of the park are outside the declared wilderness, as are the Grassy Hill and Culoul Range tracks.

If you intend to cross private land when driving into or out of the park's non-wilderness areas, you should seek permission from landholders. Visitors who fail to observe this courtesy make it harder for others later. Note that some landholders have locked gates on access tracks. If planning to use the Martindale Trail, contact *The Ranch*, ☎ 02 6547 3526 or ☎ 02 6547 3512. For the Commission Road, contact *Wongalee* at Appletree Flat, ☎ 02 6576 4034.

Appointments to view the Aboriginal rock art at *Glen Ann* can be made by contacting the property's owners, Rodney and Noelene Smith, ☎ 02 6574 5176, or the Bulga NPWS office, ☎ 02 6574 5275.

Jessie Grattan, 5, of Blacktown and friends play in Wheeny Creek, in the far south-east of Wollemi National Park. A car-camping ground here offers shady tent sites and a toilet block.

Index

Page numbers in *italics* indicate captions, but where a reference appears in both text and caption on the same page, it is shown in roman **type** only.

Aboriginal people, 17, 22, 25, 26, 46, 62, 63, *85*, 90, 101, *109*, 110, 117, 123-24, 134, 144-45,
  groups
    Darkinjang,145, 147, 152
    Darug, *109*, 117
    Dhungutti, 144
    Gundungurra, 21
    Wiradjuri, 134, 145
    Wonarua, 144-45, 147
Acacia Flat, *109,*
Alidade Hill, 152
Animals, *6*, 25, *29, 37, 45, 55-56, 97*, *129*, 134, 139, 147, 148, *149, 150,* 151
  introduced, 52-3, 56, 151-52
Appletree Flat, 14
Atkinson, Louisa, 107
Australian Conservation Foundation, 137
Australian School of Mountaineering, 88

Baal Bone Creek, 128
Baal Bone Gap, 130
Baiame, 144-145
Banks, Joseph, *104*
Barrallier, Francis, 17, 41, 46, 49, *51*
Barrett, Jim and Pat, 64-5
Bartlett, John 38
Bartlett Head, *30, 36*, 39, 41
Barton, Edwin, 102
Bass, George, 17, 102
Bathurst, 62
Bats Camp, 25, *28*, 35
Baudin, Thomas, *144*
Begg, Caroline, 48, *49-50*
Bell, Archibald, 62
Bell Range, 66
Bells Line of Road, 99, 101, 105, 112, 117, *120*, 121, 123, 126
Bellvue, *120*

Ben Bullen State Forest, 128
Bent Hook Swamp, *34*, 35
Beowang, 113
Bilpin, 118, *120*, 121
Bindook, 25, 33-5
Bindook Creek, *34*, 35
Bindook Falls, *34*
Bindook Gorge, *34*
Bindook Highlands, 35
Birds, 21, 44, *46, 58*, 77, 109, *117, 129*, 139, *142*, 151
Bishop, Peter, 91, 109
Black Hole of Calcutta, *102*
Blackheath, 66, 81, 94, *95*, 97, *104*, 111, 118
Blaxland, 66
Blaxland, Gregory, 17-18, 62
Blue Gum Forest, 105, *106*, 107, 109-11
Blue Gum Forest Committee, 109
Blue Labryinth, 63
Blue Mountains City Council, 65, 84
Blue Mountains Committee of the National Trust, *70*, 71
Blue Mountains Heritage Centre, 94, 97
Blue Mountains NP, 18, 22, 31, 35, 39, 41, 49, 63, 84, 88, 117
Bob Turners Track, *155*
Bowenfels, 79
Box Ridges, 137
Boyd, Arthur, 71
Boyd Plateau, *25, 29*, 52, *53*
Boyd River, *29*
Braeside Walk, 97
Bridal Veil Falls, *95, 96*
Brown, Ian, 53, 94
Brunet, Alfred and Effie, 118
Bulga Creek, 140
Bullaburra, 110
Burragorang, 46
Burragorang Lookout, 48
Burragorang Tablelands, 48
Burragorang Walls, *48*
Burramoko Head, 101, *104*
Butchard, Stirling, 131
Bygone Beautys, 81

Byrnes Gap, 41, 43

Caffrey, Lyndel, *91*
Caley, George, 17, *18*, 49, *51*, 102, *104*, 117
Canoe Creek, *139*, 152, 156
Capertee River, 124, 132, *133*
Capertee Valley, 130
Carrington Hotel, 81, 90, 92
Cathedral of Ferns, 114, 117
Catholic Bushwalking Club, 64
Caves Creek, 28, 31, 33
Caves House, *6*, 55, *57*, 58
Cedar Road, 43, 51-2
Chappell, John, 58
Christys Creek, 49
Church Lane, 114
City of the Blue Mountains, 18, 84, *85*
Claustral Canyon, *102*
Colo Committee, 137, 154
Colo Gorge, *139*, 152, *155*, 156
Colo Heights, *155*
Colo River, 132, 148, 152, 154
Colon Peaks Mine, 38
Colong Caves, 22, 25, 28, 31, *33*
Colong Committee, 31, 52, 154
Colong Foundation, 130
Commission Road, 140
Commonwealth Oil Corporation, *130*, 132
Confederation of Bushwalking Clubs of NSW, 101-2
Conservation Hut, 74
Cooper, Mark, 128, 130
Cooper, Maurice, 81
Cooper, Russell, 137
Coricudgy State Forest, 136
Cowparlour, 139
Cox, William, 62
Cox Junction, 44
Cox Valley, 46
Coxs River, 22, 26, 44, 46, 50, *51*, 94, 128
Crushers, The, 90
Cudgegong River, *6*, 134
Currant Mountain Gap, 136
Cusack, Dymphna, 92

Dardanelles Pass, 87
Dark, Eleanor, *88*, 91
Dark, Eric, 88
Darkey Creek, 147
Darling Causeway, *106*, 112
Darwin, Charles 17, *66*, 71, 74, 97
Daughters of Our Lady of the Sacred Heart, 81
Dawes, William, 102
de Strzelecki, Paul, *17*, 97
Deep Pass, 123, *124, 126*
Den Fenella Waterfall, 77
Devil's Coachhouse, *54*, 55
Devils Wilderness, *18*, 101
Dharug NP, 18
Dockers Ladder, 111
Doyles Creek, 139-40
du Faur, Eccleston, 107
Dunns Swamp, *6*, 134, 136
Dunphy, Milo, 31, 52
Dunphy, Myles, 28-33, 41, 43, *50*, 52, 109, 154, *155*, 156

Echo Point, *85*, 87
Edmonds, Jenni, 61, *63*
Ekin, John, *80*, 81
Ellyard, Sarah, 48, *49, 50*
Empress Falls, *10*
Emu Plains, *64*
Engineers Pass, 107
Engineers Track, 102
English, Mick, 52-3
Euroka Clearing, 63
European colonists, 17, 22, 102, 145
Evans, George, 62
Evans Lookout, *94, 111*
Everglades Gardens, 79, *80*

Fairfax Heritage Track, 97
Fairmont Resort, *85*
Fairy Grotto, 101
Falls Gallery, 71
Falls Road, 71
Fattorini, Lucien, 28, 33
Faulconbridge, 68
Federal Pass, 66, 87
Fern Tree Hill, 117
Fletcher Street, 74

Florabella Pass, 66
Folbigg, Don and Ben, *139*, 156
Follenfant, Trish, 79
Fortress Creek, *6*
Fortress Hill, *111*
Foster, David, 92
Foy, Mark, *91*, 93
Friends of the Blue Gum Forest, *109*

Gallop, Bert, 28-29, *30*, 33
Gardens of Stone NP, 18, 124, *127, 129*, 130, 137
Gentle, Max, 132
Ghent, Gary and Helen, 113-14
Giant Stairway, *85*, 87
Gingra Creek, 51-2
Gingra Range, 48, 50, 52
Glen Ann, 140, 147
Glen Davis, 132, *133*, 134
Glenbrook, 66
Glenbrook Creek, 66
Glenbrook Gorge, 63-5
Glenbrook Tunnel, *63*
Glow Worm Tunnel Road, *125*, 124
Glow Worm Tunnel, *124, 126*, 131
Gondwana Walk, 118, *119*
Gordon Creek, 79
Gospers Mountain, 132
Goulburn River NP, 18
Government Town, *36*, 39
Govett, William, *95*
Govetts Creek, 105, *106, 109*, 110
Govetts Gorge, 94, *95, 96, 102*, 111
Govetts Leap, 94, 97, 105, *111*
Govetts Leap Lookout, *95*
Govetts Leap Road, 94
Grand Arch, 31, *33, 54*, 55
Grand Canyon, 94
Grassy Hill Track, 152
Great Dividing Range, *93*, 94, 128, 130
Great Western Highway, 63, 65, 92, 97, 112
Great Western Hotel, 90
Great Zig Zag, 64, 79, 98-9
Gregson, Jesse, 113
Grose, Francis, 102
Grose Gorge, 66, 97, 101, *104, 109,*

Index

111-12, 123
Grose River, 101-2, 105, *106*, 110
Grose Valley, *6*, 110
Gurnang State Forest, 22
Gurney, Rod, 128-130

Hamilton, Trevor, *102*
Hammon, Harry, Isobel and Phil, 87
Hanging Rock, 101, *104*
Hartley Valley Four-Wheel Drive Club, 128
Hell Hole Mine, *58*
Hole-in-the-Wall Canyon, *88*
Holland, Ernest, 56
Holman, Norah, *70*, 71
Holmes-Drury, Judith, *114*
Hooker, Leslie, 37
Hooper, Ron, 81
Hopwood, John, Kiara and Lyn, *57*
Howe, John, 140
Howes Valley Creek, 139
Huber, Martina, *73*
Hughes, Robert, *69*
Hungerford, Clarrie, 105, 109-11
Hungerford Track, 101
Hunter Range Trail, 128-29, 134, 139, 142
Hunter River, 18, 139
Huntsman spider, *6*
Hydro Majestic Hotel, *91*, 92-4
Hydropathic Sanatorium, 92

Imperial Hotel, 90, 97
Innes, Paul, 92
Insects, *6*, *126*
Inspiration Point, *85*

James, William, 70
Jamison Creek, 71, *73, 74, 76*
Jamison Valley, 74, *76*, 79, *85*, 87
Jellybean Pool, 63
Jenolan, 28, *55*
Jenolan Caves, 28, *54, 55, 56, 58*
Jenolan Caves Reserve Trust, 56
Jenolan Caves Resort Pty Ltd, 55
Jenolan River Gorge, *57*
Jenolan Valley, 58

Johnson, Anthony, 151-152
Johnston Falls, 49
Joynton-Smith, James, 97
Jumpback Pass, 48
Junction Point, 44, 48

Kaar, Ashley, *26*
Kanangra, 29, 48
Kanangra Falls, *25*
Kanangra Gorge, 21, *22, 26*
Kanangra Main, *6*
Kanangra Tops, 22, 41, 49-50, 52
Kanangra Walls, 21-2, *25*, 48
Kanangra-Boyd NP, *6*, 18, 21-2, 31, 41, 49, *55*
Kanangra-Boyd Wilderness, 49
Katoomba, 21
Katoomba Falls, *66*
Kerr, Greg, *26*
King, Philip Gidley, 41, 49
Kirkby, John and Rosemary, *57*, 39
Knapsack Gully, 65
Kolonga Canyon, 101
Kolonga Labyrinth, 101
Konangaroo State Forest, 52
Kondek, Tony, 48
Kowmung River, 22, 33, 41, 43, 48, 49, *50*, 51-2, 107
Kowmung Track, 22
Kurrajong, 132

Lake Burragorang, 22, 25, 35, 41, *43, 45, 46, 48, 51*, 128
Lang, Val, *34*
Lang, Val and Neville, 33, 35
Lannigan, Edward, 28
Lannigans Creek, 29, 33
Lapstone, 64
Lapstone Creek, *64*
Lapstone zigzag, 64
Lawson, William, 17, 62
le Blanc, Lloyd, *114*
Leach, Geoff, 90, 92
Lennon, Jane, 68
Lennox, David, *64*
Lennox Bridge, *64*
Leura, 79, 81, 148
Leura Forest, *66*

Leura Golf Course, *80, 85*
Leura House, *80*, 81
Lhuede, Aubin and Val, *36, 37*, 39
Lindsay, Norman, 68-9
Lithgow, 112, 128
Little Blue Gum Forest, 107
Little Capertee Creek, 132
Lloyd, Warren, *65*
Lockley, John, *111*
Lockley Pylon, *6*, 111
Locomotive 3830, 61, *63*
Lord, Gabrielle, 92
Low, John, 65

McCauley, Andrew, *88*
MacDonald River, 139
McKeons Creek, 56
McLean, Mark, 52
McMahons Lookout, 48
McManamey, John, 70
Macquarie, Lachlan, 62
Macqueen, Andy, 102
Malaita Point, *83*
Mallitt, Mark, 44, 46
Manning, Harold, 37
Marlin, Paul, *102*
Martindale Creek, 139
Mayer, Janet, 48, *49*
Medlow Bath, *91*, 92
Meeres-Wilson, Jared, *147*
Megalong Valley, 87, 92, *93*, 94
Meldrum, Sam, 37
Mellong Swamp, 151-2
Mentzel, Britta, *104*
Meredith, Georgina and Sue, *147*
Meredith, Nicholas, 48-9, *50*, 139
Messel, Harry, 65
Miller, Max, 71
Misty Gully, *25*
Mittagong, 10
Montz, Barbara, *6*
Moody, Mary, 118
Moore, Charles, *114*
Morong Deep, 22
Morris, Glen, 140, 144-45
Mount Armour, 28
Mount Banks, *6*, 70, *104*
Mount Blackheath, *96*

Mount Blaxland, 62
Mount Cloudmaker, 21
Mount Colong, 22
Mount Coricudgy, *134*, 136
Mount Emperor, 29
Mount Midderula, *134*
Mount Solitary, 79, *80, 83*
Mount Tomah, 70, 117
Mount Tomah Botanic Garden, *10, 101, 117-18, 119*
Mount Victoria, 62, 66, 97
Mount Wilson, 70, 107, 112-13
Mount York, 62
Mountain Trails Club, 29, 109
Mud Tunnel, 58
Muir, Keith, 130, 152
Murphy, Derek, 88
Myrtle Creek, 137
Myrtle Grove, 137
Myrtle Gully Trail, 137

Narrow Neck, 21
Narrow Neck Plateau, *83*
National Parks and Primitive Areas Council, 31
NPWS, 39, 41, 46, 53, 110, 132, 136, 140
National Pass, *61*, 66, *73-4, 76*
National Trust of Australia, 69, 70, 79, *80*
Nattai NP, 18, 35, 39, 41
Nattai River, *26*, 46
Nepean River, 63, 102
NSW Electricity Commission, 154
NSW Lands Department, *110*
Newnes, 131-32
Newnes, Sir George, *150*, 132
Newnes Hotel, 131, *133*
Newnes Junction, 126, 132
Newnes Plateau, 124, 148, 154
Newnes State Forest, *88*, 124
Noble, David, 119, *123*
Norman Lindsay Gallery, 68
Norris, Frank, *36, 37*
North, John, 90
Nullo Mountain, 137

Oberon-Colong Stock Route, 25, *28*

Olympia Steps, 58
One in Four Pass, 48
Orient Cave, *57*
Orphan Rock, 87, 90
Osborne, Armstrong, 58

Pagoda Lookout, 134
Pagodas, 124, 126, *127, 129*, 134
Pantoneys Crown, *129*, 130
Paragon, The, *79*
Parr, William, 139-40
Paterson, William, 102
Paul, Bernhard, *73*
Peckman, Harry, 92
Pembroke, Thomas, 70
Perry, Victor, 140, *144*, 145, 147
Perrys Lookdown, 110, 111
Persian Chamber, *57*
Petit, Nicolas, *144*
Phillip, Arthur, 61, 102
Pierce, Bert, 105, 109
Pearces Mountain, *46*, 48
Pierces Pass, 66, 88, 105, *106*
Pigott, Peter and Ann, *114*
Pillans, Brad, 58
Pipeline Track, 132
Plateau Walk, 22
Pool of Cerberus, *58*
Prince Henry Cliff Walk, 87
Prince Regent Glen, *73*
Private Town, *36, 37*
Pugh, Clifton, 71
Putty, 147
Putty Creek, 139
Putty Road, 140, 147, 151

Queens Cascade, *76*

Raspberry Junction, 139
Rayleigh scattering, 65
Recreational Four Wheel Drive Clubs Association, 129
Red Hands Cave, 64
Richardson, Vanessa, 25, *28*, 31, 33
Richmond, 102
Rickard, Sir Arthur, 66
Rigby, Alan, 109
River Cave, 56

Index

Rocky Creek Canyon, *123*
Rodriguez Pass, 66, *111*
Rodriguez, Thomas, 66, *111*
Romilio, Mario, 81
Royal Botanic Gardens, 119
Rylstone, 134, *136*
Rylstone District Environment Society, 137

Scarlett, Phil, 35
Scenic Railway and Skyway, 87
Scotts Main Range, 43, 48, 49
Seymour, Thomas, *22*
Sharpe, Wendy, 71
Shead, Garry, 71
Sheepskin Hut, 139-40
Sheepskin Mountain, 139
Shields, Bill, *120*
Silver Mine Hotel, 37
Silver Peak Mine, *38, 39, 41*
Simos, Zacharias, 79
Six Foot Track, *54,* 55, 58
Smith, Anne, 71, 74
Smith, Dick, 154
Smith, Gordon, 132
Smith, Hardy, 28, 33
Smith, Ian, 71, 74
Smith, Noelene and Rodney, 140
Snake Mountains, 48
Soady, Rose, 68-9
Sorensen, Paul, 79, *80*
Springwood, 66
Stalagmites
    Grand Column, 58
    Mother and Child, 31
    Pillar of Hercules, *57*
Steinberg, Mathias and Kerstin, *66, 76*
Stimson, Anthony, *147,* 151
Streeton, Arthur, 65
Sublime Point, *83*
Sugar Loaf Hill, 43
Sydney Basin, 24
Sydney Bush Walkers, 109, 132
Sydney Water, 39, 44, 46, 52

Tench, Watkin, 102
Tennant, Kylie, 92

The Ranch, 139
Thompson, Patrick, 48-50
3801 Ltd, 63
Three Sisters, *6, 85, 83,* 87, 88
Three Ways junction, 139
Thurat Spires, 21
Thurat Walls, 21, *26*
Tindale, Bill and Joan, 137
Tonalli Cove, 48
Tonalli Peak, 41
Tonalli River Valley, 41
Top Points, 65
Trickett, Oliver, 28
Tuglow Caves, 22, 28
Twenty Mile Hollow, 70

Upper Burragorang Co-operative Cheese Factory, 48
Upper Kowmung Gorge, 22

Valley of the Waters, *10, 17, 61, 66, 74, 77*
Van de Velde, Henri, 79
Varuna, 91-2
Vegetation, *6, 10, 17,* 22, 25, *29, 33,* 44, 48-49, *50,* 53, 65, 66, *76,* 97, 106, 107, 109, 113, *117*-19, *124, 129,* 136-37, 139, 152, 156
    introduced, *52,* 113
Victoria Pass, 66
Vulcan State Forest, *52*

Wales, Allen, *134,* 136
Wall, Dorothy, 66
Walls Lookout, *104*
Wanganderry Walls, *45*
Warragamba Dam, 44, *46*
Warragamba Gorge, *46*
Warrimoo, 66
Washington, Haydn, 119, 136, 154
Watson, Allan, 132
Weatherboard, 79
Weatherboard Inn, 71
Webb, Cecil, 107
Wedding Cake Mountain, 137
Wentworth, William, 17-18, 62
Wentworth Falls, *18,* 48, *61, 66,* 71, *73, 76, 77, 79,* 81, 148

Whalan, James, 55
Wheengee Whungee Creek, 49
White, Patrick, 114
Whitehouse, Harry, 107
Whitton, John, 64, *98*
Widden Valley, 137
Wilderness Act 1987, 18, 43, 102
Williamson, Doug, 56
Wilson, Jeremiah, 55
Wilson, John, 112
Wilson, Sue, *88*
Wirraba trail, 129
Withycombe, 113
Wolgan River, 123, *124,* 131-32
Wolgan Valley, *124,* 126, 128, 130
Wollangambe River, 117, 123
Wollemi Creek, 152
Wollemi NP, *6,* 18, *88,* 106, 117, 121, 123-4, 128, 130, 132, 134, 137, 139, 140, *142,* 147, 154, *155,* 156
Wollondilly River, 26, 44, 46, *51*
Wollondilly Valley, 26, 46
Wombeyan Caves, 28
Wonarua Tribal Council, 140
Woodford, 69-70
Woodford Academy for Boys, 70
Woodford station, 69
Worsman, Adam and Janelle, *102,* 118, 123, 124, *126,* 128
Wran, Neville, 152, 154
Wynn-Carrington, Charles, 90
Wynne, Richard, 112
Wynstay, 113

Yarrawa, 112
Yengo, 113, *114*
Yengo NP, 18, 140, 147
Yerranderie, 28, *30, 36,* 37-9, 41, 43, 46
Yerranderie Peak, 39
Yodeller Range, 137

Zig Zag station, 99
Zigzag railways, 64-5, 99
Zig Zag Railway Co-op Ltd., 99
Zusters, Reinis, 74

FURTHER READING

Barrett, Jim *Shack Country and the Old Burragorang.* Guntawang Catholic Youth Centres, Sydney, 1990.

Barrett, Jim *Kowmung River.* Jim Barrett, Glenbrook, 1993.

Barrett, Jim *Yerranderie: Story of a Ghost Town.* Jim Barrett, Glenbrook, 1995.

Barrett, Jim *Life in the Burragorang.* Jim Barrett, Glenbrook, 1995.

Falconer, Delia *The Service of Clouds.* Pan Macmillan, Sydney, 1997.

Hungerford, M.E. & Donald, J.K. *Exploring the Blue Mountains.* Kangaroo Press, Sydney, 1982.

Low, John *Blue Mountains: Pictorial Memories.* Atrand Pty Ltd, Sydney, 1991.

Macqueen, Andy *The Life and Journeys of Barrellier 1773- 1853.* Andy Macqueen, Springwood, 1993.

Macqueen, Andy *Back from the Brink – Blue Gum and the Grose Wilderness.* Andy Macqueen, Springwood, 1997.

Meredith, P. *Myles and Milo.* Allen & Unwin, Sydney, 1999.

Mosley, Geoff *Blue Mountains for World Heritage.* Colong Foundation for Wilderness, Sydney, 1989.

Park or Pines: The Battle for the Boyd. Colong Foundation for Wilderness, Sydney, 1986.

Paton, Neil *Walks in the Blue Mountains National Park.* Kangaroo Press, Sydney, 1987.

Powell, Greg *Bushwalking in the Blue Mountains.* Rigby, Sydney, 1980.

Powell, Greg *Bushwalking through history.* Macstyle, Hampton, 1989.

Prineas, Peter *Wild Places* (2nd ed.). Colong Foundation for Wilderness, Sydney, 1997.

Smith, Jim *From Katoomba to Jenolan Caves – The Six-foot Track 1884-1994.* Second Back Row Press, Katoomba, 1984.

Smith, Jim *How to see the Blue Mountains.* Second Back Row Press, Katoomba, 1986.

Smith, Jim *The Blue Mountains – a guide for cyclists.* Wombat Outdoor Adventures, Campbelltown, 1991.

The Colong Story. Colong Committee, Sydney, 1982.

The Mount Tomah Book. Mount Tomah Society, 1987.

The NSW NPWS has a number of guides and booklets covering aspects of the Blue Mountains. These are authoritative and highly recommended. They are available from the Blue Mountains Heritage Centre, Govetts Leap Road, Blackheath.